THE
BRITISH COUNTRYSIDE
IN PICTURES

Newton Tracey, Devon

THE
BRITISH
COUNTRYSIDE
IN
PICTURES

*In four illustrated sections, each
introduced by Brian Vesey-Fitzgerald*

CONTENTS

ODHAMS PRESS LIMITED · LONG ACRE · LONDON WC2

The Countryman in His Garden. A garden is the countryman's hobby as well as a source of food supply. Contented labour is the spirit of this scene at the village of Portbury in Somerset.

Country Folk and Country Ways

THE British tradition is a way of life, a reflection of character built up through the years by a people whose homeland has been settled and well ordered during a long period of history. Amid all changes in social and economic conditions the country folk of Britain have preserved the continuity of the British tradition.

Although it is true that some of the more obvious differences between town and country have been dispelled by modern methods of communication, by migration and by universal education, a distinction between the townsman and the country-man remains; in customs, in appearance, and in speech. A great many human races, speaking divers languages, have con-tributed to the making of Britain. Quite clearly defined types reaching far back into the history of this island are to be met with regularly in the country, unaffected by the levelling tendency of the big cities.

Extreme variation in colouring is em-phasized by the blond hair and clear blue eyes of the Nordic, in strong contrast to the flashing dark eyes and swarthy complexion of those with Spanish blood. In the East Riding of Yorkshire a noticeable racial type—broad-shouldered with blue eyes and flaxen hair—still persists, a legacy from the days when Norsemen swept across the North Sea, deep into this part of England. In the Meon Valley of Hampshire, a dis-trict conquered by another invader in British history—the Jutes—one finds men of medium height, thickly built, fair-haired and blue-eyed, who might well man the inshore fishing boats of Jutland. Angles, Jutes, Saxons, Normans, these came late in the island story, driving the settled peoples westwards. Before them, the Celts were masters of England, and before the Celts, the people called Iberians, a small, dark people with long faces and aquiline noses. Through the long centuries the Iberian type has persisted: it is common in certain villages of Hampshire, Berkshire and Somerset. And more than the type per-sists. The Iberians were a pastoral people; today small, dark men are especially noticeable among those who handle sheep, horses and cattle. There are still true Celtic types on the Chiltern Hills—descen-dants of men and women who hid in the thick woods during the Norse and Saxon invasions. And in the fens of East Anglia a dark-haired, small-boned type remains, descendants of those who sought refuge in the impenetrable marshes centuries ago. And to all this must be added much foreign blood. There are Spanish types on the Scottish border—the Romans gar-risoned the wall with a Spanish legion once. A Mediterranean strain can be traced along the South Wales coast. But it is in Cornwall that this is most noticeable. The Phoenicians came to Cornwall for tin: there are certainly many Cornishmen today who might be on the waterfront of Jaffa as easily as on Falmouth quay, and there are Cornishmen with Mongoloid features, and Cornishmen who must claim somewhere in their ancestry the blood of those early inhabitants of the world.

Gypsies are a foreign race, despite four hundred years' residence. There has been much intermarriage between Romanies and country folk, and full-blooded gypsies are now not very common, but those that remain are as much members of a foreign race living in England as, say, Poles or Indians or Chinese.

To this diversity of appearance must be added diversity of language. The people are described as Anglo-Saxons. But there is a great difference in the speech, especially in the pronunciation of vowels, between Angles and Saxons. The letter " u " is the test. The short, clipped " u " of the Englishman is Saxon, and you will hear it only in Saxon districts. Long drawn out —" cup " pronounced " coop "—is Ang-lian, and you will hear it only in Anglian districts. These were the tongues of inva-ders. The ancient British mode of speech is now heard only in the West, quick and lively with a lilt to the end of it, the speech of the Welsh border counties and of Wales.

It is when the countryman discusses country crafts that dialectic differences are most marked. The countryman from the

North and one from the South may speak the same language concerning politics; but let them talk " shop " and we see the difference. Take sheep, for instance. A Cumbrian will call them gimmers, a Leicestershire man threaves, a Sussex man ewes. According to the district, grass in a hay-field may be known as fog, aftercut, eddish or aftermath.

The village is a natural focus of country life, though the picture has been altered in our time. Until recently it centred round the squire and the parson. Economic conditions have been partly responsible for the dwindling power of the squire, whilst various secular organizations supplement the activities of the Church. The everyday life of the village now centres round the farm or farms, since the farmers have become the chief employers of labour.

A good deal of social life centres round the inn, which is much more than a place in which to drink. It is a club, where men may talk, and play, discuss local politics and manage local affairs, and a good landlord is an inestimable asset to a village. There has been a noticeable increase in feminine activity in rural areas in the past generation due to the influence of the Mothers' Union and the Women's Institute. These two excellent organizations have given to the women of rural England opportunities for social intercourse and social service that were hitherto lacking. Nor has the full effect of their influence on rural Britain yet been felt.

Another institution of great value to the community is the village hall. This is a centre both of recreation and of social service. Dances, jumble sales, and whist drives are held which serve the purpose of entertainment, and are a means of support of various charitable organizations. Neither is instruction outside the classroom of the village school overlooked. Again, the hall is the setting for lantern-slide lectures and debates in which every member of the community may take part.

Though race and language persist in the face of migration, unification and education, the same cannot be said of our old country customs and relaxations. Such traditional institutions as the village cricket match, bell ringing and carol singing still hold sway. Year by year, however, cere-monial customs become fewer and fewer, and attempts by enthusiasts to revive them meet with little or no success. Morris dancing, the Mayday pole, mumming, mothering—these still go on, though they are becoming less common with modern progress. There are certain customs connected with most of the Church's festivals, but especially with Christmas; there are others connected with the seasons of the year; and there are others still that are directly connected with the land, its cultivation and its tenure. Of the last category, the best known is the fair. The country fair has a history going back to Roman times in Britain, though since there was then no charter these early institutions were not, strictly speaking, fairs, but were rather fêtes. Most of the fairs were held annually, as, for example, St. Giles's Fair at Oxford, St. Bartholomew's at Newbury, Goose Fair at Nottingham, St. Giles's Fair at Winchester, but some, such as Pole Fair at Corby, in Northamptonshire, which occurs but once in every twenty years, are periodic in character. Various customs connected with land are traditional, and are usually concerned with the preservation of some right acquired long ago by villagers or commoners. The common custom of beating the bounds is such a one, and another, less well known, is the Grovely Oak ceremony at Wishford, in Wiltshire, by which the villagers maintain their right to gather dry wood in the Forest of Grovely.

A number of old country customs survive, divorced from their original purpose, but infinitely strong traditionally, as children's games, common alike now to town and country. Ring-a-ring-o'-roses, Nuts in May, Hunt the Slipper, Hop-Scotch and Peg Top may be cited as examples. " Conkers", that game beloved of small boys and girls everywhere, is also very ancient, though its origins are not known.

But old customs are only one small aspect of the pleasant pattern of country life. As a whole the day-to-day existence of the country folk reflects a warmer personal relationship, a self-reliance and adaptation to circumstance which is being crushed out of the towns by the swiftness of progress, and although it incorporates what is useful in the new way of life, it preserves much that was best of the old.

Highland Shepherd and his Sheep-dogs. In a mountain glen, a sturdy, tweed-clad young shepherd watches over his flock. The sheep are a hardy breed and thrive upon the Scottish hills.

Harvesting in Devon

THE ROAD MENDER

THE GOOD EARTH

" *A team of horses hour by hour,*
Drags a harrow through the heavy fields:
And larks fly up from nearer meadows, sing
To larks below concealed."

A. S. WILSON.   *These Remain.*

Close to the earth is the countryman in all his daily tasks. At left is a road mender at the village of Dulverton in Somerset, engaged in cleaning and levelling one of those trim, narrow lanes which give so much beauty to the British country. Below, is a scene which might be encountered in any of Britain's rich shires, for even today, despite the increased use of mechanical devices in agriculture, horse and man still toil in their traditional partnership. The spirit of such a partnership has been beautifully interpreted by A. S. Wilson in the lines quoted above.

REAPING OATS IN ARRAN

Apple Picking in Kent. An old countryman, cheeks as rosy as the fruit he is gathering, fills his basket in an orchard. He is one of what an early English observer called " the rustic yet civilized people of Kent", who have through the ages made their county into a garden.

Snowdrop Time in Sussex. It is early in the year, a mild day in February, and the moist green earth is starred with the delicate bloom of the snowdrop. A typical village woman of Easebourne (used to much stooping in the fields) begins her collection of flowers for market.

15

THE GYPSY ENCAMPMENT

" Up the road to Romany
It's stay, friend, stay!
There's lots o' love and lots o' time
To linger on the way."
WALLACE IRWIN. *From Romany to Rome.*

The gypsies have dwelt in Britain since about the year 1500, having spread westwards from Eastern Europe during the fifteenth century. An act of the reign of Henry VIII lays down several regulations governing their behaviour. During four hundred years they have retained many of their original characteristics, for example, their swarthiness of appearance, their practice of fortune telling, their wandering habits and to some extent their language. Some who were not gypsies have been fascinated by the life and joined the roving tribe, but it still remains a picturesque race apart. The gypsies follow the round of rural events from place to place and are to be found in numbers at the centres of hop and fruit picking. The Derby, of course, attracts them each year to the Epsom Downs where this photograph of a typical encampment was taken. The caravan in the foreground is built in the age-old style and is gaily decorated.

HOP-PICKING, KENT

Camp Folk. A scene such as this is timeless in its attraction. On a mild night in early spring the gypsies have gathered round the cheerful blaze of a fire. At right is another form of primitive encampment—that of a charcoal burner in the Forest of Dean. Once charcoal burning was a flourishing industry, quantities being used for the reduction of iron from its ores. In Sussex much timber was hewn down for this purpose. Nowadays the charcoal burner still supplies some specialized needs, for example, the sticks of charcoal used by artists.

THE CHARCOAL BURNER

Village Cricket, Ickwell, Bedfordshire

Rabbiting. A countryman on the South Downs is just about to release a ferret down the rabbit hole. He has already stopped up all outlets except one. The ferret which is held on a string will then drive the rabbits to the remaining outlet. A net is ready to catch them as they appear.

The Pack Returns

Gone Away. The cry of "Gone Away" from the huntsman's leather lungs indicates that the fox has broken covert and is heading for the open country. The photograph has all the spirit

of the "Shires", where several famous packs of fox-hounds are found. The "Shires" is a recognized, if somewhat vague term for the counties of Leicester, Rutland and Northampton.

DUCK SHOOTING ON THE BROADS

From the butts built in the reeds a sportsman takes an overhead shot at a duck in evening flight. The shallow, reed-fringed lagoons which constitute "the Broads" are a great resort of birds, and Ranworth Broad, where this photograph was taken, is said to be one of the richest places in Britain in wild fowl, though shooting is controlled. Many acres are reserved as a sanctuary and are equipped with special observation posts for studying the habits of various wild birds. Horsea Mere, near Hickling Broad, surrounded by reedy marshland, is the haunt of hundreds of different species of birds. The bittern was saved from becoming extinct by its protection on an island in Hickling Broad and its numbers have since considerably increased. It is not the only bird that has been saved from extinction. Norfolk is a centre for nature study as well as sport.

THE PLEASURES OF FISHING

" *Now expectation cheers his eager thought*
His bosom glows with treasures yet uncaught.".

JOHN GAY. *Rural Sports: A Georgic.*

Fishing is an ever-popular pastime in rural Britain, has long had a social aspect in the angling club and, in Isaak Walton's *The Compleat Angler*, produced a literary classic. Apart from salmon and trout, pike, perch, carp, tench, barbel, bream, roach, dace and chub are all valued. The two fishermen shown in our photograph, absorbed in the pursuit which British writers have described so well, are standing on the banks of the River Mole, near Dorking in Surrey. The Mole comes from Sussex and flows into the Thames, though in reaches like this it seems essentially a part of the Surrey landscape. The slopes of Box Hill form a pleasant background.

29

Salmon Fishing, Selkirk, Scotland

Playing Keels. Above, in the ancient village of Lanreath in Cornwall, a game of keels is in progress. This is a simple form of the bowling game which has been played for many hundreds of years in Europe and in which the players attempt to knock down the nine pins which are set up diamond fashion.

The Innkeeper. Presiding spirit of innocent rural pastimes such as the game of keels is the innkeeper of the type seen in our photograph at right. A glass of country ale or cider is the natural accompaniment to the activities of the players and the leisurely recreation of local gossips here seen taking their ease.

THE VILLAGE INNKEEPER

The Clipping Supper. Sheep-shearing in Cumberland is known as " the clipping " and in some parts is still treated as a festival. The men of the fells come from miles around for the

work.   After it is over, the clippers take off their " kytles " or overalls, clean off the wool grease and assemble in the great stone barn where the farmer entertains them to a hearty supper.

HARVEST OFFERING

All over the world there are special
harvest customs and it has been a season
of rejoicing since the most distant ages.
In Britain as elsewhere the sheaf, once
taken to represent the corn-mother, still
retains a symbolic importance. This
picture shows farmers of the village of
Hambleden in Buckinghamshire, near
Henley, entering the church in pro-
cession with their offering of corn for the
Harvest Festival. By custom, centuries
old, they are met at the lych gate by the
choir and follow with their sheaves which
are placed on the church steps. In olden
days the corn was given to the Church
as part of the parson's wages. Tradition
decrees that should the ceremony here
illustrated be missed for one year
it can never be repeated afterwards.
In Devon and Cornwall especially, harvest time is a season of universal
rejoicing, which culminates in the traditional harvest supper at which the
farmer with his family and all the men
who have helped to bring in the harvest
give thanks for the bounty of Nature and
drink to the success of next year's crops.
In these counties, too, a number of
traditional ceremonies dating from early
Celtic times have survived. A few
such as the ceremony of " crying the
neck " at Towednack, which had previously died out, have been revived in
recent years.

BELL RINGING

"*Then let the village bells, as often wont,*
  Come swelling on the breeze.....
  It is enough for me to hear the sound
  Of the remote exhilarating peal,
Now dying all away, now faintly heard,
And now with loud and musical relapse
Its mellow changes huddling on the ear."
                        REV. JAMES HURDIS. *The Village Curate.*

This is an ancient art with a long tradition in Britain and one not much practised elsewhere. Scientific "change-ringing" was introduced in the seventeenth century and had a great revival in the nineteenth century. Ringing by hand is carried out by means of a rope attached to the bell which either moves it as it hangs mouth downwards ("chiming") or swings it round nearly full circle ("ringing"). In change-ringing, the bells are rung in a varying order by a team, the skill and effort involved being considerable. Above are bell-ringers at Alfriston in Sussex.

CAROL SINGING

"Hark! The herald angels sing
Glory to the newborn King.
Peace on earth and mercy mild
God and sinners reconciled."
CHARLES WESLEY. *Eighteenth Century Religious Carol.*

Another ancient custom is carol singing, and though this is limited neither to Britain nor to the country, it is in traditional and picturesque surroundings that it may be heard to best advantage. The origin of the word "carol", which is lost in antiquity, seems to have originally suggested a ring dance and the ceremony among other pagan rituals found its way into that of the Christian church. Old carols retain many of the features of folksong. Our illustration shows boys of the Heritage Craft School at Chailey in Sussex singing carols at the entrance to the chapel.

CONCLAVE AT THE VILLAGE INN

Words are not wasted. There are long intervals of silence while the elders of the village ponder over many and weighty subjects. The youngest of these old men of Bradford Abbas in Dorset is over eighty. The majority of them are close to ninety. Posters of local agricultural shows line the passage which leads into the parlour. An ancient skittle game stands on the table: and the wisdom of the village here finds expression in calm and serious utterance. Such inn parlours with their low raftered ceilings, their sanded floors and ancient benches form a social centre of rural districts. Unlike the larger inns which grew up to cater for travellers, the small inns and ale-houses supply a local need and are bound up with the traditions of a district just as much as the manor house or church. They have their own circle of customers, their recognized oracles and wits, their own jealously preserved rituals, and form a sort of rural club. Local politics and national problems alike are frequent topics of conversation; talk in the " local " is generally a sure guide to the temper of Britain's rural workers. Here, in short, develop in a convivial atmosphere the opinions which help to shape the nation's destiny.

Market Day (above). Lowing of cattle, squealing protests from the pigs, puzzled bleatings from the sheep, are sounds which mingle with the raucous cries of hucksters and vendors of patent cure-alls. It is market day at Malton, Yorks, and farmers from miles around have brought their livestock to market. Shrewd farmers gather round the pens, silently absorbed in mental calculations. Presently the auctioneer elbows through the throng, and his untiring voice urges on the bidding. " Going . . going . . gone", another lot changes hands.

Open-air Stores (left). While the men are gathered round the pens, the thrifty country housewife finds plenty to interest her. Fish, fruit, meat, groceries, clothes and cosmetics are all displayed on the temporarily erected stalls, as is glimpsed from this market scene at Yatton, Somerset, round about Christmas time. The market place has become an open-air multiple store. As the afternoon wears on, and closing time grows near, prices are lowered, and the cries of the stallholders grow louder as they strive to clear their stock.

THE VILLAGE SHOP

" *Great slabs of toffee that they make,*
Which urchins eye and pray for;
Divine abundance! glorious day!
We stayed as long as we could stay."
RUTH PITTER. *Romford Market.*

Infallible magnet to attract weekly pennies is the village shop, before which one may generally see clusters of sturdy children—grubby toddlers in charge of capable elder sisters—all carefully weighing the merits of the sticky sweets that they glimpse behind the window panes. The village shop is a wonderful medley of things—containing not only sweetmeats and foodstuffs but cough medicine, newspapers, print frocks—a thousand and one articles as various as can be.

The Daily Round. The Churches have always been one of the mainsprings of village life. The Rector, the Free Church Minister, and the Roman Catholic Priest, have duties which extend far beyond the holding of services. To the village folk they are friends and counsellors.

Old Friends. In all weathers the carter and his horse make their way about the countryside, delivering parcels, taking heavy loads to market. Perfect understanding exists between man and beast as they jog along the lanes.

Call to Youth (right). While their elders enjoy the peace that comes from a leisurely meal, the church bell sends the youngsters scampering off to Sunday school, where voluntary teachers give them some simple Christian instruction.

SUNDAY SCHOOL

SOCIAL LIFE IN THE VILLAGE

Women of all classes find recreation and fresh interests in the Women's Institute.   In many a village the local institute has set up stalls to sell the preserved fruits, garden produce and honey which have resulted from its activity, as is shown in the above photograph taken at Porlock. The Women's Institute movement began in Canada about the end of the last century and it was introduced into Britain in 1915. By 1917 one hundred and thirty-seven Women's Institutes were in existence and did valuable war work, especially as regards food production. In the Second World War their number had grown to nearly six thousand and once more their services in the production of fruit and vegetables came to the fore. The movement is also social and educational and has done much to bring a fuller life to the people of the countryside by its creative programme. On the opposite page we glimpse another typical cameo of village life— a fair in progress at Redbourn, Hertfordshire. Originally fulfilling the role of market, the fair is now mainly a source of fun, laughter and gaiety and a welcome break in the workaday round.

Old English Customs Still Practised.   Above is seen the strange dance of the Deermen in progress at Abbots Bromley in Staffordshire, in which a team of "Staffordshire Yeomen", in traditional costume, dance through the village, each holding aloft a pair of deer's antlers. Below, on Furry Day at Helston in Cornwall the children dance in and out of the houses singing.

Pageantry and Ceremony. Many a stirring episode of the past is re-enacted in Britain's local pageants. In the photograph reproduced above, villagers of Hadlow in Kent are seen rehearsing their part in a pageant of the county's history. Below, the village children at Ickwell in Bedfordshire dance round the maypole on May Day, traditional public holiday and festival.

THE VILLAGE SMITHY

The blacksmith's shop is one of the eternal and unchanging features of village life and his art is as old as history. The essential characteristic of the forging process is that the metal is not melted but is worked while hot enough to be plastic. The smith uses a hand-hammer and variously formed hand tools, and he relies on muscular effort in shaping the metal. His strength is proverbial and the type of country craftsman whom Long-fellow described in his famous poem is still to be found in Britain. Though the kind and amount of traffic may change and the number of horses to be shod is not as large as it was in the old days, still there is much for the smith to do. The ubiquitous presence of motor traffic has caused many of the small country smithies to become garages and repair shops. Moreover, the village smithy often performs a service of real importance to the welfare of the community by hand-ling the repair of tractors and agricul-tural machinery—a very real need for the farmer when there is no highly-specialized engineering shop in the village. A demand for hand-wrought iron articles of use has been met. At Pyecombe in Sussex where this photo-graph was taken, a speciality is the manu-facture by hand of shepherds' crooks.

53

Britain's Fisher Folk. At left is a peaceful corner in Lowestoft Harbour, Suffolk. The fishermen look out to sea for signs of good fishing weather. Above, fish caught at Brightlingsea and Mersea in Essex are towed in special crates and sold alive on the shore. Below, sole and mackerel are being landed at Brixham, long the centre of the Devonshire trawling industry.

Reminder of Old Coaching Days (above). The old Berkeley coach passes through Amersham in Buckinghamshire. No longer an everyday feature of British life such occasional revivals bring back some of the spirit of the old coaching days and coaching ways as they were a hundred and fifty years ago.

Rural Transport. In rural areas, despite the growth of motor transport, men still jog along on horseback or in horse-drawn carts. Above, left, is an Exmoor postman on his rounds, below, left, a peaceful scene in County Antrim.

THE WATER GYPSY

There are few sights more picturesque than that of the canal boat with its string of barges making its slow and peaceful way along one of Britain's inland waterways. Very much of its own kind is canal life. Not only are the canal folk distinct but their boats, gaily striped, and with panels of landscape and flowers painted in bright colours and in a quaint traditional style, are unique. Many families of canal-folk still spend their whole lives afloat, and the women share the work equally with the men. Children attend the local schools wherever the barges tie up for loading or unloading; at important canal centres throughout the country special barge schools have been established for the young water gypsies. Very few of the older bargemen can read or write, but news is conveyed to them in the towpath inns and by the lock-keepers. Horses may still be seen plodding slowly along the towpath and drawing a barge by means of a towing rope, although motor traction has steadily replaced this leisurely method. The canal boat is a cosy floating home and travels, often through beautiful country, the length and breadth of Britain. Although its steady five or six miles per hour seems very slow when compared with other methods of transport, it is still the best and cheapest for certain classes of merchandise. The journey from London to Birmingham nowadays takes less than forty-eight hours. Altogether there are some five thousand miles of canals in Great Britain, though about half of them have now fallen into disuse.

Daffodil Harvest, Scilly Isles

Off to School—Luccombe, Somerset

Town and Village

IN the story of our towns and villages lies the history of Britain—the history of more than a thousand years of monarchy, a continuity enjoyed by no other country in Europe. This, and the fact that Britain is an island, gives a special character to its towns and villages, the character of stability. History and architecture are complementary. In considering British towns and villages you cannot consider the one without the other. Together they bring to life even the sleepiest of old towns: together they add enjoyment to a tour of Britain.

Consider only the place names. The history of the land is plainly written in the names of town and village, river and hill. River names are the oldest. Thames (Thame, Tame, Teme are local variants) is perhaps the oldest, for it seems to come from no known language and may well derive from the Iberians. Axe, Esk, Usk, Exe are all forms of the Celtic word for water, which we English now pronounce as whisky. Ouse is the old English word "ooze", meaning mud. Avon is simply the Welsh word for river, and you will find it nowhere east of Wiltshire, though you will find plenty of Celtic names further east. Dover is simply the Welsh word "dyfr", meaning water. Names with "pen" are also Celtic. Pen is the Welsh for hill: you will find the word in Berkshire (Hackpen Hill), in Hampshire (Inkpen Beacon), in the Buckinghamshire hill village of Penn, and so westward in Dorset, Cornwall (where it appears also in surnames) and Gloucestershire.

Norse words occur in foss, meaning waterfall, thwaite (a clearing), fell (a sheep grazing), skal or scale (a shed), lath (a armstead) and ford, when it occurs on the coast as in Milford in South Wales, is merely the Norse "fjord". When it occurs inland, as at Guildford and Oxford, it is the Celtic word "fordd", a road. Names ending in "by" and "ham" are of Danish and Saxon origin; Chester and caster are Roman, and so on. And most names, you will notice, are directly connected with some geographical feature; with river, hill or wood.

Roughly speaking, the towns may be divided into four groups—Cathedral Cities, Market Towns, Ports and Spas. The first planning of towns in Britain was done by the Romans, who, though they frequently adapted earlier centres of population, were governed by military necessity and placed their towns at centres of communication on the great trunk roads. Many of these towns are now Cathedral Cities—Winchester, Chester, Chichester, York, Lincoln, Exeter, Gloucester are examples and they are all alike in having four "gates". They were, in other words, set at cross-roads. Yet one of the busiest of these junction towns, Silchester in Hampshire, where a great many of the old roads met, is now scarcely more than a hamlet. In Roman times these fortified military posts were also the market towns. The Romans did not colonize Britain, they occupied it. The Saxons were conquerors and colonizers, and their towns, of which we know but little, were primarily centres for agricultural trade. They took over the Roman remains, of course, but they settled also elsewhere, as for example at Buckingham and Bedford which are centres for agricultural produce. Their "burghs" were built later, as forts against the Danish invasions. From that time onward the importance of trade exceeded that of arms and the situation of towns became governed by communications. The growth of towns around abbeys and great churches, though it has undoubtedly often occurred, has usually been exaggerated. Romsey, in Hampshire, is a good example of a town growing round an abbey, but usually the abbey came because of some factor—such as market or communication—which had already given rise to a centre of population. Communications were very difficult. Roads were scarce and water transport all important, and since bridges were few and far between, places where the water was shallow enough to be forded were naturally preferred for the sites of towns. These towns were not planned, as the Romans planned: they grew. But the market towns had one thing in common, a wide street or square

Strand-on-the-Green, Kew

in which business was transacted. Excellent examples surviving today are, among others, Marlborough, Thame, Devizes, Ripon, Stamford, Amersham, Aylesbury and High Wycombe. Ports naturally grew up around advantageous harbours, and their planning, or lack of it, was dictated purely by geographical conditions. Resorts grew around particular places either for reasons of health, as in the spas, in which case they were built about a central well or spring, or as fashionable centres for the amusement and relaxation of the rich.

Towns grew with the increase in travel following the improvement in roads. Especially was this so in the eighteenth century and we are fortunate indeed that the architects of that time were men of great taste. Our Georgian architecture is beautifully proportioned and lends to its neighbourhood a quiet dignity altogether lacking in modern building. Increase in travel meant increased accommodation for travellers. In earlier days travellers and pilgrims put up at "hospitals", some of which, like "The George" at Glastonbury, the "Angel and Royal" at Grantham and "The New Inn" at Gloucester remain. The new inns built in the eighteenth century are impressive in their dignity and excellent examples occur at Ipswich (Mr. Pickwick's "Great White Horse"), Bedford, Farnham and Oxford.

The type of building naturally depended largely on local conditions. Stone was brought from Portland for building London after the Great Fire, but until recently most towns were built with local materials and a local stamp was put upon the architecture that has remained to this day. So you will find black and white buildings all along the Welsh border from Cheshire, through Shropshire, Worcestershire and Hereford into western Gloucestershire. In East Anglia you will find mainly flint, but in places timber-framing, plaster and brick as, for example, at Lavenham; in the Cotswolds building is in the warm-tinted lichen-covered local stone; in Devon it is cob and thatch and a little building in the old red sandstone; in Kent and Surrey and Sussex brick and weather-tiling and some flint from the chalk; in the North and the Midlands, the materials are stone slab and slate, and a stone belt in Norfolk.

Villages were originally the settlements of small groups of agricultural people who worked a certain, and usually small, area of land. Thus villages are not planned. In many cases they have grown up rather haphazardly around the church. In others, as, for example, Wilcox in Wiltshire, the church came after the village and was placed on the edge. But about every village there *is* a plan. It has grown up in just that place because that was the right place for it to grow. It is the land that governs the village, not the village the land. The planners were the ploughmen and the shepherds and their plans were governed by the strata of the land, by the distances to be walked, by the presence or absence of water. The oldest thing in the village is not the church, though that may be very old, it is the workable land. The land has seen great changes; from hill to valley cultivation; from open field to enclosure. But these changes, though they affected the countryman, did not destroy the reason for the village.

Just as there are regional types of town building, so there are of villages. And as might be expected these are even more individual than in the towns, so much so, in fact, that with only a little knowledge you can identify your county fairly accurately from a glance at the building of an old village. Even the thatching varies from county to county. For example, half-timber and brick: you will find this in Essex, Kent, Berkshire and Sussex. In Kent and Sussex the pattern of the front is rich, but simple; in Essex you will find slanting timbers between the perpendiculars and much ornamental work called " pargetting "; in Berkshire the style is more like that of Kent, but the bricks are frequently set in a herring-bone pattern and the upper half of the wall is hung with weather-tiling. The black-and-white building of the Welsh border counties springs from the same source, but here you will find the timber-framing decorated with rosettes and so forth. So, too, with stone building; Cotswold stone and Northamptonshire stone are very much alike, the decoration is different. There is in our village building a vigorous expression of individuality. In Britain there are towns and villages beyond compare.

Fish Street, Shrewsbury

WEST INDIA DOCKS

One of Surrey's Prettiest Villages. The village of Shere, between Dorking and Guildford, is delightfully placed between the White Downs and the woods towards Abinger and Holmbury. A picturesque approach to Shere is by way of the Tillingbourne Valley and Albury Park.

Spire and Tower. Above is the church tower of Charlwood in Surrey, a little village not far from the Sussex border. Below is the tall spire of Eynsford church. Eynsford in Kent, in the valley of the Darent, is only twenty miles from central London despite its rural air.

MAIDSTONE
FROM THE MEDWAY

One of the most picturesque views of Maidstone ("Medway's town") is seen in this photograph taken across the Medway and looking towards the Archbishop's Palace, which is said to be haunted by the ghost of the ill-fated Archbishop Cranmer. Also to be seen is All Saints' Church, a good example of Perpendicular Gothic. Maidstone is the county town of Kent, equidistant from London and Dover, and standing on both sides of the Medway, which also marks the time-honoured distinction between "Kentish men" and "Men of Kent". The former are the dwellers in West Kent, the latter are found east of the Medway. A sixteenth-century charter incorporated the town which had, however, been a recognized meeting place for the shire, under the name of Penenden Heath, for many hundred years before. Maidstone is now a busy place with cement works and various agricultural manufactures. Its paper mills are celebrated, and it is also a centre of the hopfields, its association with this trade being a tradition of long standing.

VILLAGE GREEN AND POND, CHIDDINGFOLD

In the south-west corner of Surrey as one approaches Sussex are a number of peaceful and well-ordered villages which have been very little changed or spoilt by the passage of time. The still pond with its reflections, the trim green, the steeply gabled church, the inn with its standing sign are all typical. The village of Chiddingfold, not far from Haslemere, is a perfect example of this unspoiled kind. This part of Surrey was formerly industrial to some extent. Iron was one of its manufactures and glass was made at Chiddingfold in the thirteenth century.

PENSHURST, KENT

An historic place is Penshurst, seen in the photograph at left, which lies at the confluence of the Eden and Medway. Under the Perpendicular–Gothic church are buried the remains of Algernon Sidney, beheaded in 1683 for his complicity in the Rye House Plot, the conspiracy to assassinate Charles II and the Duke of York. One of the great houses of Kent is Penshurst Place. The barons' hall dates back to the fourteenth century. Edward VI gave the property to his chamberlain, Sir William Sidney, grandfather of Sir Philip Sidney, the poet and soldier, who was born in the house.

The Canterbury Weavers. These beautiful houses overhanging the River Stour were originally the homes of refugee Flemish weavers who settled in Canterbury in the time of Queen Elizabeth. The weavers left Canterbury for Spitalfields in London during the eighteenth century.

Canterbury Cathedral. The beauty of this great cathedral needs no description. Begun in the eleventh century it was not completed (by the great central tower) until four hundred years later. Object of pilgrimage (so wonderfully commemorated in Chaucer's *Canterbury Tales*) to the shrine of St. Thomas à Becket, it is unique in its historical and venerable character.

Dover Castle. Significant of the traditional status of Dover as a fortress and port for the Continent is the famous castle, parts of which incorporate Roman brickwork. One of its notable features is the Norman Keep whose frowning walls date back to the time of Henry II.

Cinque Ports and "Ancient Towns". Dover, Hastings, Hythe, Sandwich and New Romney were the five or " cinque " ports, once providing ships for the royal fleet. To these were added Rye and Winchelsea. Above is the Mermaid Inn, Rye; below, Black and White Street, Sandwich.

The Quay at Bosham. Bosham is one of the oldest places in the neighbourhood of Chichester, Sussex, city of ancient associations. Saxon kings lived at Bosham, and the church is of Saxon construction. The picturesque quay as seen in our photograph stands at the head of a creek.

Reflections at Aylesford.   Aylesford, near Maidstone in Kent, is a large riverside village, situated on the Medway. The bridge reflected in the placid stream is one of the five Tudor bridges across the river. The Perpendicular church stands on an elm-covered knoll of ground.

IMMORTAL CHURCHYARD

At left is the gate to the church at Stoke Poges in Buckinghamshire which attracts a constant stream of pilgrims, because of the famous *Elegy Written in a Country Churchyard*, which it inspired. Stoke Poges was for a long time the favourite resort of the poet Thomas Gray, and it was from Stoke that, in 1750, he sent to his friend Walpole " a thing to which I have at last put an end". This was the immortal *Elegy*, one of the most often quoted poems in the whole of English literature. The poet was buried beside his mother in Stoke Poges churchyard.

ANCIENT STOCKS

At the triangular green of the village of Aldbury in Hertfordshire, where four roads converge, stand the stocks seen in the photograph below, reminder of old crude punishment and summary justice.

Milton's Church. In Buckinghamshire, between Amersham and Windsor, is Chalfont St. Giles, where Milton had his cottage during the plague years, 1665–66, and where he quietly worked on *Paradise Lost* and *Paradise Regained*. The village church he attended is seen here.

Windsor Castle from the Thames. Central feature of Windsor's skyline is the massive
round tower raised on an artificial mound, on whose flag turret the Union Jack or Royal

Standard is raised according as the sovereign is absent or present. Site of a stronghold since Anglo-Saxon times, Windsor became the chief residence of royalty during the Norman period.

Venerable Churches. Opposite, above, is Winchester Cathedral from the Close. Winchester dates back to Roman times, and the Cathedral is the longest mediæval church in existence. The city has an ancient ecclesiastical history. The capital of the Saxon kings, it was also a religious centre before the Norman conquest, but the Saxon abbey church was demolished in 1079 and a great new building on Anglo-Norman lines begun. It was not until the fourteenth century that it was transformed into its present style, first by Bishop Edington and then by William of Wykeham, the celebrated founder of Winchester College and New College, Oxford, who showed such generous enthusiasm in planning and building. William of Wykeham is responsible for the conversion of the nave into a triumph of Perpendicular Gothic. Outwardly, however, the cathedral is plain. Also on the opposite page is the hamlet of Fingest in Buckinghamshire whose glory is its Norman church tower. Below are the imposing remains of the Norman abbey church at Malmesbury, a quiet little town with a fine position on a hill, on the borders of Wiltshire and Gloucestershire. The Norman abbey dominates the town and is celebrated for its south porch which is considered to be one of the outstanding examples of Norman architecture.

SALISBURY CATHEDRAL FROM WEST HARNHAM MILL

" While Salisbury stands the
test of every light,
In perfect charm and perfect
virtue bright."
ANNE, COUNTESS OF WINCHELSEA.
A Nocturnal Reverie.

The magnificent proportions of the spire of Salisbury Cathedral, the tallest in England (404 feet), can be fully appreciated in this view from the water-meadows of the Avon—a view made famous by the art of the great landscape painter, John Constable, with whom Harnham Mill (dating from the fifteenth century) is linked in fame. Salisbury Cathedral was built on a virgin site between 1220 and 1250, and though the spire in the Decorated style was added about a hundred years later, it is assumed to have been allowed for in the original plan. Certainly, the general effect is one of complete harmony, indeed one of the most superbly ordered compositions to be found in any of the Gothic cathedrals.

Market Cross, Chichester. Chichester in Sussex, a typical cathedral city, had its origin in Roman times when it was called Regnum, its name being changed to "Cissaceaster" after the Saxon invasion. The highly ornate market cross which is shown above was built in 1500.

Great Barford, Bedfordshire. In this photograph the River Ouse has overflowed its banks, and laps close against the churchyard wall of Great Barford with picturesque effect. The Ouse, as Cowper says, " slow winding through a level plain," rises in Northamptonshire, flows past Bedford, Huntingdon and Ely and so into the Wash. Ouse is one of three rivers so named.

FREEFOLK, HAMPSHIRE

St. Albans Under Snow. The cathedral of St. Albans, in Hertfordshire, is seen on a wintry evening from the River Ver. Its Norman tower was constructed mainly of Roman bricks about 1080. St. Albans adjoins the historic site of the Roman Settlement at Verulamium.

94

Summertime, Thurleigh. The drowsy warmth of a summer's day in an English village is well conveyed in this photograph of the little village of Thurleigh in Bedfordshire. The meadows are dappled with flowers and the village children have come back in triumph with posies.

The Charm of Wiltshire (left). This old cottage embowered in trees with its trimly thatched roof, its dormer window and its lime-washed walls stands near Chippenham. It amply conveys the undisturbed rural beauty of which the inland county of Wiltshire provides many examples. The distribution of population in the county is based on the rivers—of which the chief are the Thames, Kennet and the Somersetshire and Salisbury Avon—and the low ground beside them, the uplands being largely deserted. It is in these valleys that one finds delightful specimens of cottage architecture. Part of Wiltshire comes within the stone belt and some villages and cottages are constructed of this material, though good examples of brickwork are also to be found. The county is famous for many stately mansions of the seventeenth century such as Wilton, with front by Inigo Jones. Its cottage homes are equally expressive of Britain's history.

In the Heart of England. This pleasant scene is on the River Ouse, where the village of Hemingford Grey in Huntingdonshire comes down to the side of the water. Looking past the boathouse and the rows of punts, one sees the church on the very edge of the stream. The church spire was blown down in a gale during the eighteenth century and is supposed, according to local legend, to be at the bottom of the river. It has not been recovered nor has it been replaced.

Corfe Castle. One of the most impressive ruins in Britain is Corfe Castle in the district called the Isle of Purbeck, Dorsetshire. The castle, which guarded a gap in the line of hills, was built in the twelfth and thirteenth centuries. King John used it as a residence and it was a stronghold of the barons against Henry III. During the Civil War it withstood a long siege by Parliamentary forces but was eventually taken and dismantled. At the foot of the hill on which the castle stands, and on the southward side, is a charming stone-built township or large village.

98

Shanklin, Old Village (above). The Isle of Wight has many features of interest in a small space. Shanklin is one of its most attractive watering places.

Shaftesbury, Dorsetshire (below). The street goes steeply up the hill on which Shaftesbury is set, giving a widely spreading view over the Vale of Blackmore.

Buckland-in-the-Moor, Devon

Beautiful Devon Villages. Ashprington (left) occupies a beautiful position between Totnes and Dartmouth in the valley of the Dart. The river scenery of this district is famous. The steep, cobbled street of Clovelly, the celebrated Devonshire coast village in a cleft of the hillside off Bideford Bay, is seen below. It affords a delightful vista towards the furze-covered downs.

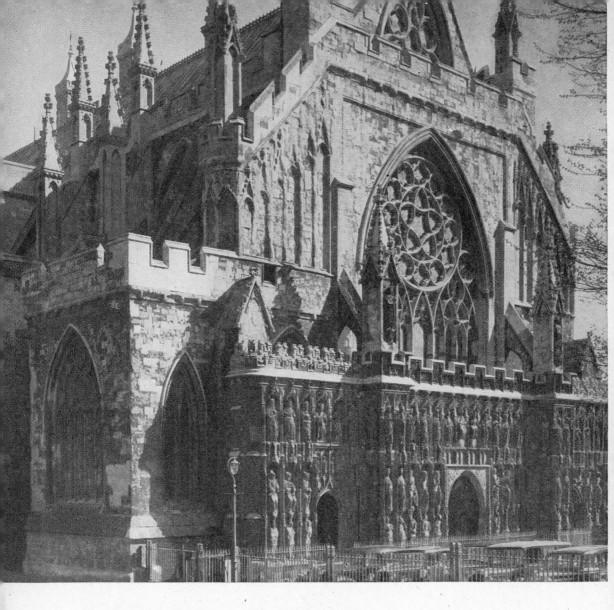

CATHEDRAL CITIES OF THE SOUTH-WEST

The photograph above shows the west front of the cathedral at Exeter, county town of Devon, the Caer Isc of the Ancient Britons and one of the most ancient towns in the country. The foundation of the cathedral dates back to 1050 when the see of Devon and Cornwall was transferred to Exeter from Crediton, but the greater part of the existing structure was built of grey stone in the course of the thirteenth and fourteenth centuries. The west front is notable for the tracery of the windows, the main window being particularly intricate and imaginative, while in the gable is a curved triangular window. The entrance screen dates from the latter half of the fourteenth century and has three tiers of sculptured kings, saints and angels, though these have been much damaged and restored. The piers of the nave were worked at the Purbeck quarries at Corfe and shipped by sea up the Exe to Topsham. On the opposite page is the modern cathedral of Truro. Truro, long the chief commercial town of Cornwall and centre of its mining industry, became a city in 1876 when the diocese was founded. The cathedral, consecrated in 1887, and finally completed in 1903, is designed in the thirteenth-century Early English style. Like other examples of the Gothic Revival, it has been criticized adversely in comparison with the Gothic of the Middle Ages though it is certainly dignified in its effect.

Beauties of Cambridgeshire. Below is the great Chapel of King's College, Cambridge, noted for its stained glass and fan-vaulted interior. At left is Ely Cathedral, built in the twelfth and thirteenth centuries, with its lantern tower and octagon seen from "Ely Porta", the stone gatehouse through which the precincts are entered. Ely is noted for its originality of design.

Villages of East Anglia. Above is a cheerful group of cottages trimly thatched with plastered brick walls, at Arkesden, Essex. Below are some of the delightfully proportioned plastered houses at Kersey in Suffolk. This village was formerly a thriving centre of the wool trade.

Village Street, Finchingfield. Finchingfield holds pride of place among the villages of West Essex. From the village pond with its white painted rails, one looks up the sloping street, along a harmonious but varied row of gables towards the grey tower of the church on the hill.

Paycocke's Hall, Coggeshall. In the main street of Coggeshall in Essex is this rich piece of half-timbered building, a fitting memorial of the prosperous merchant of the sixteenth century when the cloth trade was still flourishing. It contains superb examples of linen-fold panelling.

Plastered Houses at Ipswich. A wealth of decorative detail is to be found on the façades of sixteenth-century houses at Ipswich, county town of Suffolk, which testifies to the influence of Flemish craftsmen. Ipswich is endeared to Dickens's readers by Mr. Pickwick's visit.

Elm Tree Hill, Norwich. Norwich, the county town of Norfolk, still remains the capital of East Anglia. The old houses seen in our photograph are of the type beloved by the painters of the Norwich school. Behind, is St. Andrew's Hall, a fifteenth-century monastic building.

128

Lincoln Cathedral from Exchequer Gate. Lincoln has an ancient history, for as *Lindum Colonia* it was one of the important Roman posts in Britain. The thirteenth-century Cathedral has a commanding position on the crown of a hill in the midst of picturesque old streets.

A QUIET CORNER
OF EAST ANGLIA

The old village of Thorpe, seen in this illustration, lies a little to the east of Norwich, near the River Yare, and its situation has all the quiet charm of the flat lands of East Anglia, whose waterways hold out the promise of placid explorations to the cruising yachtsman. Within twenty miles of Norwich are the rivers and broads, or lagoons, famous as the Norfolk Broads and forming, with a few others in Suffolk, over two hundred miles of navigable waterway. These are now used mostly by pleasure craft although a few trading wherries still convey goods between town and village and the Yare itself is navigable by sea-trading vessels as far as Norwich. The broads are formed in many cases by a widening stretch of river or else by the enclosure of a sea estuary between sand banks. Several of the broads, for example, Hickling Broad, are very shallow and need dredging to keep a navigable channel. The beauty of these reed-fringed waterways is one of the great attractions of this district. Gathering the reeds and drying them for thatching is a local industry of some consequence in many parts of the Broads country.

Field of Hyacinths, Spalding, Lincolnshire

"Boston Stump" (right). St. Botolph's Church at Boston in Lincolnshire is noted for its tall tower nearly three hundred feet high and visible for many miles of flat country around. It is generally known as Boston Stump. The American city of Boston was founded in 1630 by emigrants from Boston, Lincs.

Blidworth, Nottinghamshire. Below is a typical scene of English country life in a little village of Nottinghamshire. Although this is not a district celebrated for its village buildings, Blidworth possesses a quiet dignity of its own.

The Old Stanley Palace, Chester. Chester is in itself a compendium of British history, for, as its name suggests, it was originally a Roman military station and preserves today the aspect of a walled city of the Middle Ages. Above is one of the finest of its old houses of Tudor days.

Beauty in Stone. Chipping Campden in Gloucestershire is here seen through the arch of the seventeenth-century Wool Hall, and an attractive glimpse it is of the houses of Cotswold stone along the one broad thoroughfare leading the eye towards the fine Early Perpendicular church.

Lichfield from the Cathedral Pool.   Lichfield in Staffordshire, renowned as the birthplace
of Dr. Johnson, possesses the lovely old cathedral, known as " Queen of the English Minsters".
The three spires of the cathedral, the Ladies of the Vale, as they are called, are seen here.

Milldale, Derbyshire. The scenery of Derbyshire is romantic, with its woodlands and grassy dales and streams. Milldale, the pretty village seen in the photograph here reproduced, has much of this romantic character. The stone walls of the cottages blend into the landscape.

KNARESBOROUGH, YORKSHIRE

THE SHAMBLES, YORK

Historic City of York. At left and on this page are two views of the capital of Yorkshire; the picturesque Shambles, opposite, which still consists mainly of butchers' shops and, above, the great Cathedral, known as the Minster, a unique treasury of fourteenth-century stained glass.

143

Richmond, Yorkshire, from the River Swale

DOWNHAM, LANCASHIRE

DURHAM

Northern City and Town. Grandeur and simplicity distinguish northern England rather than the mellow picturesqueness found in the south. Durham, rising above the River Wear, is unrivalled. Below is the Moot Hall and market place at Keswick, close to Derwentwater.

Home of Scottish Kings. Stirling Castle is here seen on its precipitous rock overlooking the Forth. Forming the natural gateway to the Highlands, its strategic importance is indicated by the numerous battles between Scots and English of which it was the scene in the old days.

150

Athens of the North. This is Princes Street, Edinburgh, looking westwards from the Scott Memorial. Middle, left, is the National Gallery of Scotland. The predominant architectural character of the first Scottish city is the classicism of the Regency and the great Robert Adam.

IN ABERDEEN HARBOUR

At right, behind the vessels at their winter moorings, can be seen the spires of the Townhouse, Marischal College and Citadel of Aberdeen. Aberdeen is the fourth Scottish city in population, industry and wealth. Its famous university consists of King's College, founded in 1494, and Marischal College in Broad Street, founded in 1593 by George Keith, fifth Earl Marischal. For many centuries Aberdeen has been the cultural centre of northern Scotland. It is also a great centre of the fishing industry and its activities include fish curing, shipbuilding and marine engineering. Its papermaking industry, which the water-power of the River Don has contributed to build up, is of considerable importance.

KIRKCUDBRIGHT
FROM THE RIVER

From the River Dee we have a glimpse of one of Scotland's best-loved beauty spots—the royal burgh of Kirkcudbright, with the ivy-clad ruins of Bomby Castle, founded in 1592 by Sir Thomas Mac-Lellan, at the end of the principal street. The town is rich in its ancient associations with the long border strife between England and Scotland, and the ruggedness and variety of its surrounding countryside has been the inspiration of painters and poets—including Burns. Not far from the town is the ruin of Dundrennan Abbey where Mary Queen of Scots slept her last night in Scotland. The stones of the abbey have long provided a quarry for the district.

Tobermory (above). This little port, whose harbour was built in the late eighteenth century, is the capital town of the Island of Mull. Tradition has it that a Spanish treasure from one of the wrecked ships of the Armada lies at the bottom of the harbour though efforts to find it have been unsuccessful. The little town has the general Scottish characteristics with its row of houses fronting on the road beside the harbour wall, its kirk, and the frugal Georgian simplicity of its style of building to which the white-painted frames of the windows lend a decorative note. It stands on an almost land-locked bay.

Oban (right). Oban on the western sea coast of Argyllshire has been termed the " Charing Cross " of the Highlands. It is the point of departure for many of the steamer routes of the west coast, connecting numerous islands. The interior of Lorne, of which Oban is the chief town, is moorland but the coastal region is fertile and is amply provided with rolling wooded hills. By water one can appreciate its sea lochs which break the coastline and the many little green islands which adjoin it. Trawlers, steamers and yachts use Oban harbour. The photograph reproduced opposite shows the lovely setting of the town.

Coastal Towns and Villages of Scotland. The Scottish coasts, which are deeply indented, comprise a great many inlets and bays and are dotted fairly closely with a fishing population. Opposite, above, is the quay of the fishing village of Port Gordon in Banffshire on the north-east coast of Scotland; below, Kilmuir in Inverness-shire. Stonehaven (above) in Kincardineshire, on the east coast of Scotland, is a thriving port and county town. Below is Inverary, overlooking Loch Fyne, county town of Argyllshire, though it has only about a thousand inhabitants.

THE FERRY,
ISLE OF ARRAN

Behind the ferry boat is to be seen the village of Corrie which takes its name from a rugged hollow in the hill of Am Binnein which rises to a height of over two thousand feet in the background. The photograph gives an adequate impression of the grandeur of Arran's scenery. It is the largest island of the county of Bute, at the mouth of the Firth of Clyde, being about twenty miles long and eleven miles wide. Many beautiful glens are to be found amongst its mountains. Of these glens the most renowned for their beauty are Glen Sannox and Glen Rosa divided by a narrow ridge which connects the peaks of Goatfell with its neighbouring heights. The northern hills which ascend from the moors of the southern half of the island overlook the mouth of Loch Fyne, one of the largest sea inlets of the western coast. The great variety of the scenery has made Arran world famous—the heather moors, precipitous rocky hills and the wild grandeur of the coastline. Although most of the land is unfertile and yields but a poor livelihood in return for the dour labour of the husbandman, there are well-stocked trout streams in the uplands; blackcock and grouse and some red deer are found on the island, while the people rear cattle and sheep in considerable numbers.

Crail Harbour, Fifeshire (above). The architecture of this village on the Fife coast is both sturdy and elaborate, its stone-built houses, with their stepped gable ends, rising from the massive quay in the foreground to the upper village where there is an old Tolbooth tower. The coast, at this point, is marked by shallow cliffs and rocky ledges interspersed with bays and coves rimmed by sand.

Historic Island of Iona. (Opposite) above, the mails are landed at Iona. This small and treeless island, situated off the Ross of Mull, has very few inhabitants. It is, however, of undying interest, because of its association with the early days of Christianity in Britain. Here, in 563, the Irish monk Columba founded the monastery from which his missionaries carried their religion to the mainland. Iona became " the luminary of the Caledonian regions", as Dr. Johnson said, " whence savage clans and roving barbarians derived the benefits of knowledge and the blessings of religion". Several ecclesiastical monuments remain, including cathedral, twelfth-century priory church and Celtic crosses.

Lerwick. (Opposite) below, is seen the capital of the Shetland Isles, whose link with Scandinavia goes back to the time of the Vikings. Lerwick was formerly noted as a whaling port and fishing is still the principal industry of the place. It is a town of considerable interest with its twisting streets and alleys.

Conway, Mediaeval and Modern. Conway Castle, seen at left, is not only impressive in appearance, but is considered to be the best example of thirteenth-century military engineering.

162

Beside it are the works of the modern engineer—the suspension bridge built by Telford in 1827 and the tubular railway bridge over the River Conway built by Robert Stephenson in 1848.

Towns of Wales. Above, little more than a village, is St. David's in Pembrokeshire. The cathedral stands in a sheltered valley and close by are the ruins of the palace built by Bishop Gower in the fourteenth century. Below is Llangollen, beautifully situated on the River Dee.

On the Welsh Shore. Above is the little seaport of Amlwch in Anglesey, once busy in shipping ore from the copper mines of the Parys Mountains. Below is New Quay in Cardiganshire, a miniature seaside resort on a curved bay, with a fine stretch of sand and a background of hills.

Near Ballymena, Northern Ireland. This photograph gives a typical section of north Irish
landscape in the county of Antrim—a district bounded by mountains and descending into

166

fertile valleys towards the River Bann. Linen and flax provide local industries. The low-roofed one-story cottages, or cabins, so general in Ireland, contrast with the varied cottages of England.

LONDONDERRY

Alum Bay, Isle of Wight

The British Landscape

"ENGLAND'S Green and Pleasant Land". We all know the quotation. We all accept it as true, and then think no more about it. In point of fact that famous quotation is an understatement. Britain is much more than "a green and pleasant land", it is one of the most beautiful islands in the world. Comparatively few of us realize it. If we were asked to name beautiful islands, few of us would think of Britain. Of Tahiti, yes; of Bali or Trinidad or Capri, even, perhaps, Ireland, but of Britain, no. Yet it is one of the most beautiful islands in the world.

It is very small, of course—much smaller than we realize. There is no place in Britain that is more than three hours' motor drive from the sea. Fortunately the physical features of our land are in proportion to its size. There is no really large river, no really high mountain, no large expanse of plain or forest, of marsh or lake. But there is an immense variety. Something of everything is packed into a very small area. And in this lies one of the chief charms of Britain. It is a land of surprises. Nowhere else in the world will you find so many contrasts within the space of a fifty miles' journey. But it is also a land of moderation, of compromise. None of these contrasts is so sudden as to be startling. The towns do not suddenly commence and as suddenly stop, as is the way of continental towns. They simply emerge from, and fade into, the countryside. The mountains do not jut abruptly from our plains, as is the way with so many continental mountains. The ground just swells upward. So in a fifty miles' journey across Britain you will find the land change, the birds change, the flowers change, the buildings change and the people change, even the character of the hills change, but all this change will be so gradual that you may never put a boundary to it in any one place. Yet, gradual, sometimes almost imperceptible as it is, the change is always definite, the contrast quite distinct.

A country of surprises. For example, Somerset is a land of meadows and gentle rounded hills. Yet, in the midst of it, around Glastonbury, is a fen country as typical as the fens around Cambridge and quite foreign to the character of Somerset. A few miles further and the rounded hills give place, gently but definitely, to high, bleak moorlands. Exmoor may be largely in Somerset, Dartmoor wholly in Devon, they might as fittingly be in the North. Then the Rheidol Valley in Cardiganshire: level in the swelling bosom of her hills, a green chequerboard, such as you would expect to find in the English Midlands, but not in the Welsh mountains. It is always surprising to find that eastern Lincolnshire looks like Holland, just as it is surprising to find rough heath country in East Anglia or tucked into the South Downs at Hastings.

It is impossible adequately to describe the landscape of Britain. Landscape is a matter of atmosphere, of colour. It cannot be captured in words. It may be photographed—excellently and beautifully as this book proves—but what it means, its spirit, the memories and feelings it evokes, these things vary for each one of us. The beauty of the country is due to these factors: the great variation of the soils, the climate, and the works of man's hands. The variety of weather within the bounds of a temperate climate and the enormous diversity of soils and rock formations, closely hedged about as they are by the seas, account for the uniqueness of the landscape and the soft beauty of its colouring. But this landscape has been moulded by man. And it is really because the men who have lived and worked in Britain have, until recently, been artists faithful to the spirit of the land they have worked that Britain is so beautiful.

Roughly speaking, it took man 4,000 years—from about 2,000 B.C. to about A.D. 1840—to make, or rather to remould, the landscape of the island. And throughout these 4,000 years this landscape has been changing. There is no such thing as a permanent landscape. Land always goes forward or goes back: it never stands still. That cannot be too strongly emphasized. The beautiful landscape photographs in this book are photographs of particular places at particular moments. If photographs were to be taken at exactly the same places, at exactly the same time, a year hence, every one would show some change. Now this change of landscape is caused by two factors, the working of Nature and the working of man. An excellent example of the working of Nature is to be found in the British coastline, which, so far from being a permanent feature, changes from week to week. Cliffs fall down, shingle is added to one part and removed from another. The cliffs of Suffolk, Norfolk and Yorkshire are crumbling into the sea, and the same is true of some of the chalk cliffs of the south coast. On the other hand, the cape of Dungeness gets a few inches nearer to the French coast every year. Chesil Beach (the largest shingle bank in all the world) alters in size and shape with every tide. Rivers alter also. The Wye has changed its course within quite recent years and the old course may be seen clearly. The river mouth at Cuckmere in Sussex, has changed position twice comparatively recently. The Trent and the Great Ouse are always doing this sort of thing. Even mountains do not remain steadfast. The face of Snowdon has altered; and that is true of all mountains everywhere. Rocks fall away: in some small crevice of soil a tree will take root and battle to life though all the conditions seem to be against it.

But the changes wrought by man are tremendous in their speed and extent compared with those made by Nature. Within the past hundred years parts of the British countryside have changed beyond recognition. We can all think of examples of this within the past twenty years. Suburbs have sprung up on what was once good farming land. But this sort of thing is small compared with what happened in the closing years of the eighteenth, and the opening years of the nineteenth century. Southern Lancashire was a moor bordered by mosses and sandbanks; Essex was the busiest and one of the most heavily populated areas of England, the granary of the country; the West Riding of Yorkshire was a harsh and inhospitable land, the people lived in the East Riding. Leeds was a hamlet, Beverley an important town. The industrial revolution altered the face of Britain. Much that was traditional was swept away. For the past hundred years people have been busy undoing the noble work of their ancestors. In few other countries in the world has commercial greed wrought such havoc. And if you do not believe that, think for a moment of the number of societies and councils and associations that have sprung up of recent years to protect this, and preserve that, of rural Britain. From what?

You cannot divide the landscape of Britain according to county boundaries, and even the broader divisions of north, south, east and west are not very satisfactory. No, the British landscape, always allowing for surprises, falls more naturally into areas that pay no attention to county boundaries. Something after this fashion: the country of weald and down (Kent, Sussex, Surrey and Hampshire); the chalk country (Wiltshire, Berkshire and the Chilterns); the West country (Devon, Somerset and Cornwall); the limestone country (starting in Dorset and running in a sweep over the Cotswolds and up into Northamptonshire); the Fen country of East Anglia; the grass farming lands of the English Midlands; the Welsh borderlands of hills and valleys, big rivers and " magpie " building; the Wales of mountains and valleys; the moors, dales and wolds of Northern England; the mountains, lakes and fells of Northern England; the Scottish Lowlands and the border land; and the Scottish Highlands of mountain and loch. Even these very broad divisions are not wholly satisfactory. Cornwall, for example, is West country beyond a doubt, yet it has little in common with Devon and Somerset; scenically it has a closer affinity with Pembrokeshire in South Wales. In the North, moor and mountain, wold and dale are very closely interwoven. And in Wales there is a considerable difference between the valleys of the south and those of the north owing to the incidence of coal-mining in the former. But taken over the country as a whole these divisions hold good. You are as obviously in chalk country at Dunstable as you are at Pitton in Wiltshire, despite the broad Thames Valley between: you are as obviously in limestone country at Oundle in Northamptonshire as you are at Chipping Campden in Gloucestershire. Plynlimon, the great mountain

172

HENLEY-ON-THAMES

in central Wales, could be nowhere but in Wales. It has none of the characteristics of the Cumbrian mountains, of the Pennines or of the Scottish Highlands. Ben Nevis is as typically Scottish as Snowdon is Welsh. And though it is true that Dartmoor might be on the Scottish border, or the country round Glastonbury, in Cambridgeshire, these are the surprise packets that are typical of Britain and do not spoil the truth of the general picture.

None of the rivers are really large rivers, but some give that impression. They are in proportion, and in proportion to Britain, the Severn is as large as the Amazon in proportion to South America. Severn, Wye, Thames, Welsh Dee and Scots Dee, Tay and Spey, these have all the characteristics of great rivers. The Thames is a majestic, slow-flowing river, typically English : Trent and Great Ouse, and the Sussex Arun, have something of the same character. The streams of Dartmoor are as the becks of the borderland, but the chalk streams of the south—Test and Itchen and Meon—could be nowhere else in the world.

So with the mountains: in height they are small. They would be foothills in many parts of Europe. But they are real mountains; they are not hills. A mountaineer may climb two or three peaks in Snowdonia, and men lost may die. You can take a car and drive all round the Peak district of Derbyshire in a morning, yet search parties not infrequently have to go out to search for lost climbers. It is all in proportion. Things are done on a small scale, but they are done well. In so small an island one is surprised that any one can get lost. But there are stretches of the Scottish Highlands as wild as parts of Siberia, where you may see no man nor any sign of human habitation in all of two days walking, where red deer roam freely and the golden eagle soars above. For that matter there are stretches of moorland in Yorkshire that seem trackless and unexplored—yet big industrial towns are but half an hour distant. There are no great woods left in Britain today, no forest of wood. The forefathers of the race cleared away the great woods. But there are some fair-sized, in proportion, woodlands, and there is a multitude of trees standing singly or in small groups, studding the hedgerows and lining the river banks. So that, standing on Leith Hill and looking over the Weald one gets the illusion of looking over endless forest, as indeed the Weald once was. Similarly, standing on Stinchcombe Hill and looking over the Severn Valley one sees only trees, an apparently endless forest. In fact, the word forest has nothing to do with trees; it means wild country where game is not enclosed. Wold and Weald, which are the same word, though the former has come to mean an open down, while the latter has retained its original meaning of land thickly wooded, come from the Welsh "coed", a wood, and the country where these names survive was country which was once heavily, almost impenetrably, wooded. Undoubtedly many of the hills which are now bare and open were once heavily wooded up to a height of a thousand feet. In the Lake District you may still see groups of durmast oak growing in the wildest and bleakest places, relics of a once heavily wooded land. And place names show how wooded the high ground once was. The highest point in Berkshire is called Ashdown, situated in the Vale of the White Horse.

And so, if one were asked to name the chief characteristic of the British landscape, one would answer "trees". Heather, maybe, for the Scottish Highlands, but trees for Britain as a whole. Elm in the Severn Valley, elm and oak and willow and many others for the Thames, beech for the Chilterns and the chalk country generally, pine in the little hills of Surrey, juniper and thorn on the rolling South Downs, ash and birch on cold uplands, alder climbing up wet hillsides, willow lining streams, chestnut fringing roads in suburbs, oak everywhere. Agriculture gives to the land a special pattern, the hedgerows outline that pattern and give it distinction. The people of the past built so well that their cottage homes seem to be built into the land rather than on to the land, and their use of local material made a blend not a blot; all these things, and the seas around them and the temperate climate to weather them and lend them soft colour, go to make up the landscape of Britain. But take the trees from Britain and you would take away the character. These features combined make the island, veritably, "a green and pleasant land".

174

SHROPSHIRE FIELDS

On the River Rib, Latchford, Hertfordshire. Pleasant is this summer vista of one of Hertfordshire's many streams, overhung by a canopy of willows, the surface spangled with weed swaying in the current. A considerable industry in this county is the growth of watercress.

Broxbourne Mill, Hertfordshire. In ancient times Hertfordshire derived its wealth from the rural manors with their water-meadows, fisheries, and water-mills. It is still noted for its picturesque mills of which Broxbourne provides a fine example in its setting of summer green.

BURNHAM BEECHES

In the Thames Valley near Slough is the large stretch of woodland generally known as Burnham Beeches, formerly the centre of a wild tract of heath and woodland stretching from Iver Heath to Taplow. These woods are peculiar in that the trees have been pollarded and have grown into all kinds of fantastic shapes. The strange effect of these gnarled and twisted trunks may be seen in our photograph. It is estimated that some of the trees in Burnham Beeches are as much as eight hundred years old, which means that they were growing in the days when the Plantagenet kings ruled England. The woodland is about four hundred acres in extent and since 1879 has been preserved for public use by the Corporation of the City of London, a wise step in view of the extensive suburban growth of the metropolis. Stoke Poges is near by and Burnham Beeches was a favourite resort of the poet Thomas Gray during the periods he spent at the village he made famous by his celebrated " Elegy Written In A Country Churchyard ". Burnham itself is a large and growing village, possessing one of the largest flint churches in the country. Yet another link with England's past is formed by the remains of an Early English abbey, which was founded as long ago as 1265.

The Thames at Shepperton. A good way of appreciating the full beauty of Thames scenery is to journey in one of the river boats, seen in the above photograph, nearly a hundred miles

between London and Oxford. With its luxuriantly wooded banks, its little islands and back-
waters, its gay villas and its variety of pleasure craft the Thames is a cheerful and lovely scene.

Apple Blossom in Kent

THE GARDEN OF ENGLAND

Kent, the first of the ancient English Kingdoms, has preserved its still earlier British name, and was already agricultural when Julius Cæsar landed at Deal in 55 B.C. Some of its orchards are of great antiquity and Kentish pippins have been famous since time immemorial. The photograph on the opposite page gives an effective impression of the splendour of its apple trees in blossom. The oast houses, so typical of the Kentish landscape, also remind us that it is a great country for hop cultivation, and each year sees an invasion of hop-pickers from London. Above is a scene on the wide-spreading pastures of Romney Marsh, which comprises a large stretch of flat land between Hythe and New Romney and where sheep rearing is a considerable industry. This immense flat is seamed with ditches. Within historic times it was in great part covered by a sort of vast estuary or inlet of the sea, but a continual accretion of land has gone on which led in course of time to the decay of Romney, Winchelsea and Rye from the importance they had as ports in the Middle Ages. Romney Marsh is now protected by a sea wall. The garden county as a whole has a long and varied coastline, being one-half surrounded by the sea, making it one of the most popular holiday centres of the British Isles.

Bodiam Castle (above). Romantic in appearance is Bodiam Castle, by the River Rother in Sussex, with its round towers and its wide moat, on which the swans sail with dignity. It was built in 1386 by Sir Edward Dalyngrudge, who fought in the French Wars, and his arms appear on the north gateway. Bodiam, one of the latest examples of the fortified dwellings of the Middle Ages, was carefully restored by the late Marquis Curzon, who wrote its history.

Landmarks on the Sussex Downs. On the opposite page, above, is the ancient earthwork called Chanctonbury Ring, situated on the Sussex Downs near Steyning. Flints indicate the presence of Stone Age man and there are traces also of a Roman settlement. Below is the " Long Man of Wilmington", near Alfriston, a figure which is cut into the chalk of the Downs in outline.

The Pine Country of Surrey. Firs and pines, heath and common are characteristic of Surrey, which is not a fertile county, although picturesque where still wild. The photograph above

shows the hamlet of Friday Street, near Dorking, which is to be found in a narrow wooded valley in the Leith Hill district. The valley opens to a wide pool, and is fringed by cottages.

HAMPSHIRE TROUT STREAM—LATE AUTUMN

" Where the mantling willows nod,
From the green bank's slopy side . . ."

JOHN CUNNINGHAM. *A Landscape.*

Hampshire's rivers flow from the Downs which traverse the north of the county. Thus the Meon makes its way from Petersfield by Fareham to Portsmouth Harbour; and similarly the Itchen and the Test flow from Winchester and Stockbridge to Southampton Water, while the River Lymington waters the New Forest—a real forest of trees and heath in the natural state, little altered since the time of William the Conqueror. Fertile and well-wooded, the county is also noted for the excellent fishing to be had in its rivers. The shallow, clear waters of many streams such as that shown below, provide the sportsman with an abundance of trout between March and October. The trout streams are commonly restocked from time to time.

ON THE BERKSHIRE DOWNS

" The air is cold above the woods:
All silent is the earth and sky,
Except with his own lonely moods
The blackbird holds a colloquy."

R. HENGIST HORNE. *The Plough.*

The centre of the county of Berkshire is occupied by the broad-backed Downs, which are related to the Marlborough Downs on the west and to the Chilterns. Clay, occurring together with the chalk of the Downs, makes arable cultivation possible. In fact, the county is mainly agricultural, and a very large proportion of its area is productive. The air is crisp and clear, and the rolling Downs, of which this photograph gives a typical view, present a lovely sight at any time of the year, either when the rich brown surface is ploughed up or when rippling crops of wheat and oats extend as far as the eye can see—broken by stretches of woodland and lonely farms.

Bratton Camp, Wiltshire. The outstanding beauty of Wiltshire is the " landscape of the uplands, an ocean of rolling grass . . . suddenly frozen as it were into green cliffs, whose pastoral

escarpments guard the valleys and vales like giant fortifications". The description by the late Robert Byron, aptly fits prehistoric Bratton Camp, whose ramparts overlook a great expanse.

191

Silbury Hill (above) is one of the memorials of the past for which Wiltshire is remarkable. It is situated on the edge of the Bath Road near Avebury (famous for its megalithic circle of stones) and is the highest artificial mound in Europe. Tunnelling has revealed no clues as to the reason for its erection—though it has been said that it is similar in purpose to the pyramidal mounds of ancient Mexico, and that sacrifices were performed in the view of a watching multitude. All that can be said with certainty of its age is that it is pre-Roman, as it forces the Roman road to make a detour round it.

Stonehenge (below). The general layout of this wonderful monument of the Stone Age can be appreciated from this photograph. It originally comprised two circles and two rows in the form of a horseshoe. The great stones were smoothed and shaped and some of them were imported from Wales, for reasons unknown. It may have been a temple for the worship of the sun, and retains a great impressiveness in its present broken form. About two miles from Stonehenge is "Woodhenge", first observed from the air, which consisted of seven concentric rings of posts, wooden, instead of stone.

Decoy Heath, Dorset. After a stormy day the sun sets in gloomy splendour over Decoy Heath —made famous by Thomas Hardy as Egdon Heath in his great novel *The Return of the Native.*

194

He saw in the heath neither grandeur nor cheerfulness but a symbol for the expression of his
sombre fatalism. The photograph fitly expresses the solemnity of the " enormous Egdon Waste ".

On the Banks of the Avon. This peaceful scene is in the Limpley Stoke Valley near Bath, Somerset. The River Avon flows through the north of the county which is very varied in the character of its scenery from water-meadows, haunted by devoted fishermen, to rough moorland.

Tarr Steps, Exmoor. In a deep, wooded valley in Somersetshire, near the Devon border, this ancient bridge, the oldest in Britain, crosses the River Barle. Some archæologists consider that it belongs to the time of the ancient Britons. It is held together by the weight of stones.

PORLOCK WEIR, SOMERSET

"Nigh Porlock town—O it is great
That strip of channel sea,
Backed with the prime of English Arcady!"

T. E. BROWN. *Lynton Verses.*

The village of Porlock, backed by the shaggy slopes of Exmoor, is a little more than a mile from
the sea and its port, Porlock Weir, where this attractive scene was photographed. This region
abounds in grand scenery. Dunkery Beacon, the highest point of Exmoor, lies only four or five
miles to the south and the view from the summit is considered to be the finest in the west country.
Approaching Porlock, either from Lynton or Minehead, on the edge of Exmoor, there are
beautiful views across the Bristol Channel and looking towards the coast of South Wales.

IN THE CHEDDAR GORGE

Few natural features in Britain are more widely renowned or often visited than the Cheddar Gorge, south-west of the town of Cheddar, in Somerset. It is a natural canyon, a quarter of a mile long, driven through the Mendip Hills, and its limestone cliffs reach a height of over four hundred feet. Although it attracts such a number of visitors it retains a lonely majesty. The long cleft is probably the trace of an ancient series of underground waterways, the thin top crust of which collapsed at some distant period, thereby revealing a species of gigantic tunnel. Stalactite caverns of this neighbourhood are equally famous for their extraordinary effects of form and colour and their underground streams, Cox's and Gough's Caverns being the best known. Human remains discovered there show them to have been used in prehistoric times. There is also evidence of Roman settlements at Cheddar from coins and other relics found.

A Devonshire Slate Quarry. Although most of the slate used in the British Isles comes from North Wales, North Devon also provides a quantity and this picture shows the side of a Devonshire quarry where slate, a fine-grained rock of clay substance, lies exposed. The slate is removed by means of machines which make cuts in the face of the rock and enable the material to be dislodged. It is then split, the direction of the natural cleavage producing thin slabs.

BLACKPOOL SANDS, DEVONSHIRE

" *O sweet September, where the valley*
Leans out wider and sunny and full,
And the red cliffs dip their feet and dally
With the green billows, green and cool."

F. T. PALGRAVE. *The Golden Land.*

This fine stretch of shore in South Devon is very characteristic. Here are the pines and firs growing near the sea, the wooded combes and steep hills, the reddish soil and the golden sands, which together endear the coun.y to so many people. The sands have an air of quiet seclusion and make a good bathing place, and Blackpool (near Stoke Fleming and Strete) has historical associations. Here Warwick the Kingmaker is said to have landed during the Wars of the Roses.

Old Cottages, Bryanscombe, Devon. The termination "combe" signifies a depression among hills and is common in the undulating country of Devonshire. Set on the edge of a little stream crossed by a rustic bridge, these cottages at Bryanscombe nestle under the lee of the hillside.

Land's End. The granite cliffs of England's most westerly point, Land's End, in Cornwall, thrust out into the Atlantic. It is set in magnificent coastal scenery and pounded continuously by the sea. From it, on a very clear day, it is possible to see the Scilly Isles, twenty miles away.

Cotswold Country—near Stow-on-the-Wold

COTSWOLD FARM, COWLEY

Bibury, Gloucestershire. The photograph above shows the famous Arlington Row at the village of Bibury in the Coln Valley on the Cirencester-Burford road. Bibury is so scattered that it resembles a series of hamlets but the great poet and designer, William Morris, whose own village of Kelmscott is so beautiful, declared it to be the loveliest village in England. The gabled and dormered cottages, pictured here, backed by tall trees, form a composition in stone. Bibury attracts anglers as well as connoisseurs of rural architecture.

The Dignity of Cotswold Stone. The Cotswold Hills form a limestone plateau which divides the Thames Valley from the Severn and this region is famous for the beauty of its towns and villages. It has been justly said that there is no part of England where the houses, built of blue-grey stone, with mullioned windows and stone roof slabs, fit more naturally into the landscape, and they provide convincing evidence of the old principle so much lost sight of in modern times, that local materials are the most suitable for building. The stone is of the finest quality and both the photographs reproduced here display its charm.

207

Haunt of Wild Birds (above). The flat lands of eastern England and especially of East Anglia with their lonely stretches of fen, river and coast are a great haunt of bird life and here the scientist and photographer have ample opportunities for observation. It is to be noted that Britain led the way in the protection of birds, and, apart from the preservation of game birds on behalf of the individual landowner, was the first country to introduce general legislation, on grounds partly of the usefulness of birds in destroying insect and other pests, and partly because of the beauty and interest of particular species. In the photograph above a watcher is intent on the study of the short-eared owl.

On the River Stour (at left). This is a scene on the estuary of the Rivers Stour and Orwell near Harwich. The sailing barge, *Resolute*, drives along before a fresh breeze. The name " barge " was originally applied to a small sailing vessel, though it afterwards came into use for any flat-bottomed boat carrying goods by water—but on tidal rivers and for coasting purposes barges are still provided with masts and sails, like the sturdy wooden vessel shown in our photograph. The great billowing clouds, the low coast line, the picturesque lines of the craft together convey the authentic atmosphere of the east coast.

FLATFORD MILL, SUFFOLK

Flatford Mill is one of the hallowed buildings for ever associated with Britain's great men, for it is the subject of one of John Constable's masterpieces, " Flatford Mill ", painted in 1817, when the artist was forty-one years of age. Constable was born at East Bergholt and his father owned water-mills at Dedham and Flatford as well as two windmills. As a youth, John worked in the counting-house of the family milling business, and in maturity he depicted with intimate knowledge the country in which he spent his early years and for which he retained a deep affection. Essentially, the " Constable country " is the lower valley of the River Stour, which divides Suffolk from Essex and flows by Flatford Mill itself. Here are the flat stretches of meadowland, the willow-lined streams and the expanse of sky which are so distinctive in the painter's work. In such pictures as " View on the Stour ", " Dedham Vale ", " The Cornfield " and " The Haywain ", Constable has given a perfect expression of the homely and unpretentious beauty of this countryside. East Anglia has been one of the main fountainheads of British art. In addition to Constable, Suffolk can claim Thomas Gainsborough who was born at Sudbury on the Stour and who also had a life-long affection for this landscape.

Post-mill, Thorpeness, Suffolk. The windmill, visible from afar on downs or in open flat lands, is one of the traditional landmarks of the British landscape, although, since the first half of the nineteenth century, it has yielded place to steam power and the windmills which survive are mostly of historic interest. The example shown in our illustration is a German or post-mill (Germany and Holland having first provided the two types most commonly found in Britain). In the post-mill the entire building revolved on a central post, shifting the mill to get the benefit of the prevailing wind, while in the Dutch mill the building remained stationary, only the roof revolving according to the wind direction. In both, the sails and wind wheel were similar. The mills of Suffolk provided inspiration for the painter John Constable, and are a special feature of the " Constable country " in whose radius the photograph shown above was taken.

NORFOLK SCENE

" And there, below the elm-tree shroud,
Where shaded air might cooler swim,
There lay a quickly-panting crowd
Of sheep, within the shadow's rim."

REV. WILLIAM BARNES. *Sheep in the Shade.*

Since the Domesday Survey, Norfolk has been noted for its flourishing sheep farms. Special mention was made in the county record of flocks numbering as many as 1,300. The expanse of flat land combined with the nature of the rich loam soil, gives good pasture to the short-wool species. These sheep bear short, dense wool of very fine quality, and make excellent mutton. The most prevalent breed, the Suffolk, had its origin in 1790, when Southdown rams were crossed with ewes of the black-face Horned Norfolk. This gave the Suffolks their distinctive dark faces and legs. The group below was photographed on the Norfolk-Cambridgeshire border.

Approaching Storm, Norfolk Coast

Tintern Abbey and the Wye Valley

Beautiful Setting of Historic Buildings. The builders of the past had an unerring eye for the appropriate site. Tintern Abbey (opposite) in a meadow on the bank of the Wye, and Ludlow Castle (below) on its hill, are two unrivalled examples of monastic and military planning.

HORSESHOE BEND OF THE WYE

The valley of the River Wye, which rises
on the eastern slope of Plynlimon and
eventually joins the estuary of the
Severn, is outstanding for its scenery and
it would be difficult to match in any part
of the country the spectacle afforded by
the magnificent curve of the stream seen
in the photograph at right. Near
Whitchurch is the famous beauty spot,
Symond's Yat (or Gate), and opposite
lies the Yat Rock, at the neck of a great
loop which the winding river here takes.
From its summit there is a wonderful
view. Between Goodrich, below Ross,
and Chepstow lies that part of the river
where the scenery is at its most beautiful.
Along this unrivalled stretch of the Wye
stands Tintern Abbey, perhaps the most
romantically situated monastic ruin in
the British Isles. Only the roofless nave
and walls now remain of this abbey,
which in bygone centuries was one of the
richest Cistercian houses with a great
company of monks. Tintern Abbey by
moonlight is a beautiful spectacle. Below
Tintern comes the Wyndcliff, rising
sheer above the Wye and thickly
wooded. The summit of the Wyndcliff
gives views along the river which are
surpassed only by those from Yat Rock.

Border Castle, Whittington, Shropshire. Whittington Castle is a stronghold of the Middle Ages, whose ruins stand in the village of Whittington, five miles from the Welsh border. It was once a seat of the Peverils. Its battlemented towers, reflected in the moat, still withstand decay.

SHROPSHIRE HARVEST FIELD

The rays of the setting sun paint the yellow harvest with warmer colours and throw ever lengthening shadows across the field. The scene is typical of many a harvest landscape in Britain, and Shropshire itself is largely an agricultural county, four-fifths of which at least are under cultivation. Barley and oats grow in the sandy soils and loams of its northern districts, wheat on the western and southern sides while the cultivation of sugar beet has also been developed.

In the Welland Valley (above). This scene in the valley of the River Welland which divides Lincolnshire from Northamptonshire, with its willows and lush grass, is an epitome in itself of the peaceful beauty and rich pasturage of rural England. The grazing herd has a sleek and well-fed look that is entirely in keeping with the trim and sunny character of the landscape. They are " beef cattle", Hereford bullocks, and the district is considered to provide the best fattening pastures in the country. The Welland flows from Northants to the Wash.

Charnwood Forest (opposite). Charnwood Forest presents a striking contrast to the lowland picture above. It is a rocky and hilly tract of land in Leicestershire which extends over an area of sixty square miles. Its trees and boulders are diversified by stretches of heather, gorse and bracken, and to the walker its scenery extends an irresistible invitation. In this district one finds Bardon Hill which rises to a height of nine hundred feet, the ruins of Augustinian priories (Ulverscroft, Grace Dieu) and Mount St. Bernard, modern Cistercian Abbey.

222

DOVEDALE, DERBYSHIRE

Midland Landscape. At left is the valley of the River Dove, between Derbyshire and Staffordshire, whose wooded shores rise to bare steep hills. In contrast with this natural landscape is the industrial scene of the Staffordshire Potteries, though this has its own picturesqueness.

Duddington, Lincolnshire. There is an air of serenity and peace about this view of meadow and stream in the neighbourhood of a little Lincolnshire village, typical of a county which is

almost entirely agricultural. Lincolnshire is one of the principal grain-producing districts and is also the second largest county in England, with an area of 2,646 square miles.

Crowland, Lincolnshire. One of the gracious features of the British countryside is the combination of natural beauty and historic monuments—such as Crowland Abbey, here seen embowered amid sprays of blossom. The abbey's chief remains are west tower and north aisle.

Tree-lined Walk. The River Wharfe flows through the moors of Wharfedale, with the ruins of Bolton Abbey a mile from the village of Bolton Bridge. Alongside it is a pack-horse road.

FLAMBOROUGH HEAD (right)

This great chalk headland on the north-east coast rises to a height of four hundred feet, and forms the northern extreme of the great chalk belt which extends across Britain and the southern extremity of which is marked by Dorset. The neighbourhood is the haunt of large colonies of puffins, guillemots and other sea birds which lay their eggs in the ledges and crevices of the cliff face. Egg-gathering is one of the occupations of the people of Flamborough, Bempton and Speeton, and they are lowered perilously down the side of the cliff by ropes, to collect the eggs, and carry off the young birds. Between Flamborough and Scarborough the Yorkshire coast is at its best.

WHITBY FROM SANDSEND (left)

On this grand stretch of the Yorkshire
coast stands Whitby, famous as a holiday
resort, for its red-tiled fishermen's cottages and for the ruins of Whitby Abbey,
where, in Saxon times, Cædmon, " father
of English sacred song", was a monk.
The Abbey is just visible in the centre
background of the photograph. Inland
are the moors and along the coast by way
of Sandsend and the Saltburn road are
the picturesque fishing villages of Runs-
wick Bay and Staithes, with their clusters
of houses steeply descending to harbour
and shore, and somewhat resembling
the little coastal villages of Cornwall.

231

BARDEN TOWER, YORKSHIRE

A LAKELAND FARMSTEAD

" Embrace me, then, ye Hills, and close me in:
Now in the clear and open day I feel
Your guardianship; I take it to my heart;
'Tis like the solemn shelter of the night."

WILLIAM WORDSWORTH. *The Recluse*

The road to the farm goes on a little way, then stops short as it comes to the boulder-strewn foot of the hills. The scene is above Coniston Water on whose shores lived the great writer and nature-lover, John Ruskin. The Coniston Fells rise to heights of between two and three thousand feet. The isolated mountain farms, with their suggestion of hard but contented industry, inspired Wordsworth to much moving poetry, still more their background, as in the lines quoted. A feature of this country is the stone walls which here replace hedges. There is a real art in building these walls of which a good example is to be seen on the left in our photograph.

Glen Ridding. This is a characteristic view of the rugged country of Westmorland, and the mountain stream brawling among the rocks, with a background of steep slopes, has all the desolation and majesty of which Wordsworth wrote with so much appreciation. It is not surprising that the economic development of Westmorland has been slow and unimportant, for the rocky nature of the ground has not favoured agriculture, while lovers of unspoiled nature may rejoice that the lack of fuel has hampered the growth of manufactures. A large proportion of the land under cultivation is pasture. The loneliness of this scene is emphasized by statistics which show that Westmorland has long had fewer than a hundred people per square mile.

SNOWSTORM, NEAR SKIDDAW

Views of the Lake District. Above is a spur of the Helvellyn Range, which forms a background to a "shieling", mountain shelter for sheep and shepherds; below, Ullswater, one of the chief lakes of Westmorland, together with Haweswater, Grasmere, Rydal Water, and Windermere.

Jesmond Dene. This wild and romantic dene, or valley, forms a public park in Newcastle-on-Tyne. Its beauty is in striking contrast to the busy industrial life of Tyneside, a few miles distant.

Landmark of Roman Britain (opposite). One of the principal antiquities of Britain is the Roman Wall, built in the time of the Emperor Hadrian (A.D. 117-138) to protect the settled land from the northern barbarians. It extends from Bowness and the Solway Firth to Wallsend on the estuary of the Tyne, a distance of about seventy-four miles. The wall was a fortified sentry beat and Roman legionaries paced the top, eight feet wide, where the pedestrians of today take their excursion. The wall linked a series of forts and was designed for purposes of observation rather than as an invulnerable defensive work.

Bass Rock, Firth of Forth (below). Thirty miles north of the Scottish-English border is the Bass Rock, which stands adjacent to North Berwick in East Lothian at the entrance to the Firth of Forth. It is a squat, grass-covered promontory a mile out to sea, celebrated as a haunt of wild birds, being a favourite breeding ground of gannets, whose nests are found in its ledges.

ANNANDALE, DUMFRIESSHIRE

View from Stirling Castle. Stirling Castle marks a transitional point from Lowland to Highland country and in this view from the castle one looks over the meadows of the Forth

244

towards the slopes of the Ochil Hills. The Castle is approached from the esplanade on which stands a colossal statue of Robert Bruce. Near the town is the famous battlefield of Bannockburn.

245

EVENING, LOCH LOMOND (right)

This view of the largest and most famous of the Scottish lochs, between Dumbarton and Stirling, is taken from the southern end where it becomes a broad sheet of water, fringed by low wooded shores and dotted with small islands called "inches". Towards its northern end the loch narrows and, like so many others, is hemmed in by mountains, for a distance of some fourteen miles. Ben Lomond, over three thousand feet high, appears on the right of the photograph. This, the most southern of the Highland mountains, marks the transition to Lowlands.

246

A PEAK OF GLENCOE (left)

Here is one of the rocky hills which tower above the famous glen in the north of Argyllshire. The mouth of the glen is on Loch Leven and its bed is swept by the River Coe, which rises at its eastern end. On both sides it is hemmed in by precipitous heights which contribute to the gloomy impression it makes, though its grim character is traditionally associated with the massacre of the Macdonald clansmen in 1692. Macaulay, writing of this historical event said: "The progress of civilization which has turned so many wastes into fields yellow with harvests or gay with apple blossoms has only made Glencoe more desolate".

Castle Campbell and the Ochil Hills

Ben Nevis. Above is a winter view of the highest mountain in the British Isles, Ben Nevis, which rises to a height of four thousand four hundred feet. In spite of its height its contours are not as precipitous as might be expected, although its bulk is imposing enough. From the summit, which is reached by a well-defined track and a fairly easy climb, there are panoramic views of the mountain scenery of the western Highlands. The top of Ben Nevis is crowned by an observatory now disused. On the western side of the mountain is pine-clad Glen Ben Nevis, which extends along the course of an ancient glacier.

Scottish Mountain and Loch. At right, above, is a view of Loch Shiel and the Glenfinnan Hills and, below, Beinn a Bheitir, from Camas a Chois, North Ballachulish. Loch Shiel is a long stretch of water between Inverness and Argyllshire, and Loch Eil and the coast. It was on its shores that Prince Charlie raised the standard of rebellion in the Forty-five, and a monument still commemorates the spot. Loch Leven narrows at Ballachulish in Argyllshire and a ferry joins up the road between Inverness and Glasgow. The hill-slope where the " Red Fox " Campbell of Glen Ure was murdered in 1752 appears in the photograph. These stretches of gleaming water, hemmed in by lofty mountains, and often deep, are a characteristic aspect of Scottish scenery.

SPEYSIDE, INVERNESS-SHIRE

SUNSET, LOCH ASSYNT

Among the many lochs of Sutherland, the largest is Loch Assynt. It has a beauty of its own, which does not depend on any natural luxuriance, for it has not many trees, but is due partly to its colour, the blue of the water on a sunny day contrasting with the brown of the moors and the purple of the hills. It is ringed round by a number of mountains, Ben More, the highest point of the county, which rises to a height of over three thousand feet, the Quinag, and to the south the peaks of Canisp. Loch Assynt, outstanding among a great number of lochs and tarns, is six miles long, two hundred and eighty-two feet at its greatest depth and two hundred and fifteen feet above the sea level. It contains a number of small islands. Sutherland, despite its northerly situation, was the " Sudrland " or southern land of the Scandinavian colonists of the eleventh century, so called in relation to their settlements in Shetland and the Orkneys. It is an unproductive area. Only one-fortieth of Sutherland is under cultivation, the shire ranking the lowest in Scotland in this respect. Most of the surface is grazing ground and wild deer forests.

RIVER LOCHAY, PERTHSHIRE

The inland county of Perthshire, the fourth largest in Scotland, is very mountainous and among its well-known heights are those made famous by Sir Walter Scott's *Lady of the Lake*, Ben Ledi, Uam Var, Ben Venue and Ben A'an, while to the same literary source is due the fame of its lakes, such as Loch Achray and Loch Katrine. In addition there are many lovely glens among which Glen Artney, Glen Almond and Glen Lochay may be mentioned. The last is illustrated below with the waters of the River Lochay rushing turbulently over the rocks. In such districts are found not only red and roe deer, but game birds in plenty, capercailzie, ptarmigan, woodcock, grouse, while the unpolluted water of the rivers abounds with salmon and trout.

RELIC OF MEDIEVAL SCOTLAND

The earliest stone castles in Scotland were the thirteenth-century keeps of Norman adventurers. These took full advantage of natural strong points and were enclosed by walls with towers at the angles. Examples of such castles are Bothwell, Inverlochy, Dunstaffnage and shown above, Kildrummie Castle in Aberdeenshire, a stronghold which has stirring associations with the days when the rivalry of Celt and Saxon was at its height in the time of Edward I. On one of his expeditions to the north, triumphal and more or less warlike marches to overawe the unruly nobles, Edward halted in 1303 at the castle of Kildrummie, prior to taking up his quarters for several months at Aberdeen. The long train of armoured knights, with their gay banners and arms flashing, advanced in gorgeous cavalcade towards the walls which are now a hoary ruin. The castle was then held by Robert " the Bruce", not as yet avowed enemy of the English (in the following year he supported Edward in the capture of Stirling) though later he was to march to Scone and become enthroned King of Scotland. The castle is still impressive in its decay.

Near Kinlochbervie, Sutherlandshire. This rocky and barren landscape with its stone walls, one-storied cottages and distant mountains is a typical aspect of Sutherland. It is a county of crofters and many holdings are under five acres. Oats, barley and potatoes are cultivated.

A JURA LANDSCAPE

WINTER SUN, SCALLOWAY (right)

This is a view of the ancient capital of
Shetland, the group of islands which
constitutes a county of Scotland and is
also the most northerly British possession
in Europe. Invaded by Norsemen in the
eighth and ninth centuries, the islands
have retained many Scandinavian characteristics, names and phrases of Norse
origin being common. The coasts are
deeply indented, so much so that no
point of the land is more than three
miles from the sea. Scalloway, on Mainland, the largest of the hundred islands
or islets which compose the group,
stands at the head of a bay, its pier and
the warehouses connected with the fishing industry being silhouetted in our
photograph against a wintry sunset glow.

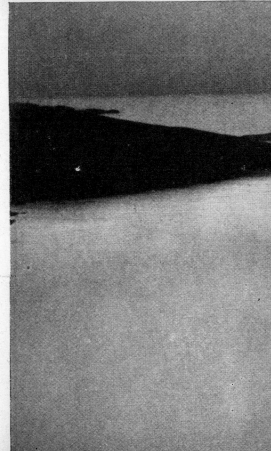

OFF THE ISLAND OF MULL (left)

This volcanic island is the largest of the Inner Hebrides, Argyllshire, and is noted for its basaltic cliffs and granite hills. Its highest mountain is Ben More, referred to as the " cloudiest hill in the Highlands." Mull possessed various small clans, prominent among whom were the MacLeans, who were great adherents of the Stuarts and took part in the risings of 1715 and 1745. Gaelic is still spoken there. The population has been dwindling, and the only town is Tobermory, which has about eight hundred inhabitants. This town, built in the eighteenth century, has declined since its early days with the removal of the herring industry. The damp climate of the island suits it better for grazing purposes than the cultivation of crops.

THE FISHING FLEET RETURNS

The waters round her broken coastline provide Scotland with one of her most valuable industries—trawling. The boats of the great northern herring fleet, some of which are seen in this photograph, land on an average nearly four million hundredweights of gleaming herring each year. Much of the catch is cured or preserved, but a proportion of this very large quantity of fish is rushed south by special train to be sold as " good, fresh herring " in a multitude of shops and stores. Scotland abounds in small fishing ports, of which the most famous are Buckie, Montrose, Stonehaven, Banff and Cromarty on her east coast; and Stornoway, Barra, Lochinver, Ballantrae, and Inverary on her west. In addition to these principal seats of the trawling industry mention must be made of the hardy islanders of Orkney and Shetland, who have trawled the narrow seas for hundreds of years, father handing down his craft and knowledge to son.

Glen Rosa, Isle of Arran. This is one of the loveliest glens on the island of Arran. The sharp, snow-covered peak of Goatfell rises in the background, in tremendous majesty, to a height of 2,866 feet. Round the coast of this island, however, there is a margin of lowland.

Llanberis Pass, Snowdon. Surrounding the peak of Snowdon are Aberglaslyn Pass, Rhyddu Pass and the Pass of Llanberis, one of the wildest and most awe-inspiring of the Welsh valleys. The road from Llanberis to Capel Curig winds among its glacier-borne boulders in a desolation broken only by the wires and pylons of the electricity grid. From this road a turn to the right leads to Beddgelert. At the foot of the Llanberis Pass is the picturesque village of Old Llanberis. A railway ascends from Llanberis to the top of Snowdon, a distance of $4\frac{3}{4}$ miles.

Harlech Castle, Merionethshire

At the Head of Glyn Collwn, Breconshire (opposite). This photograph was taken in the wild mountainous country near the South Wales coalfield between the Black Mountain of Carmarthenshire and the Black Mountains of Breconshire, where the Brecon Beacons, bare and steep, descend to fertile valleys intersected by mountain streams and waterfalls. Here is a view looking across the lovely Glyn Collwn towards the source of the River Caer Fannell, a tributary of the Usk. A waterfall, Blaen-y-Glyn, can be seen near the farm.

Dinas Mawddwy, Merionethshire (below). This village, situated on the upper Dovey, was once the seat of the independent lordship of Mawddwy and also the haunt of a band of red-haired robbers who terrorized the district until put down during the reign of Henry VIII. The village lies cradled among the mountains and is a convenient point from which to climb the Arans which lie about five miles to the north and whose peaks overlook Snowdonia.

In the Valley of the Ceiriog (opposite). Here is Llanarmon Dyffryn Ceiriog along the Glyn Valley, or valley of the Ceiriog, in the Berwyns. In this neighbourhood there is a tablet to the memory of Thomas Jefferson, draftsman of the American Declaration of Independence, whose ancestors emigrated from the Snowdon country in the seventeenth century—not the only American association of this part of North Wales, for the ancestral home of the founder of Yale University, Plas-y-Yale, is not far away on the Corwen-Chester Road.

Swallow Falls, Bettws-y-Coed (below). These falls, called Rhaiadr-y-Wennol, occur where the River Llugwy cascades over a broken cliff and are famous for their beauty. The district around is studded with many gems of scenery, and the village of Bettws-y-Coed itself, surrounded by trees and murmuring waters, is considered to be without rival in North Wales. The landscape painter, David Cox, discovered its attractions more than a century ago, and painted a signboard for the " Royal Oak," which is still preserved there.

Aberglaslyn Pass. Above and opposite are two aspects of this celebrated gorge at Beddgelert, Carnarvonshire, through which runs the River Glaslyn. On each side are crags and cliffs clothed with larch and pine trees. The view, above, was taken from the bridge over the Glaslyn.

272

Distant View of Snowdon. Snowdon, called Eryri, or " Eagle height " in Welsh, is the highest mountain in England and Wales. It has five peaks, and corries and lakes to the east and south.

Past and Present in Wales. Above is the little seaside resort, Aberdovey, or Aberdyfi, which stands at the mouth of the estuary of the Dovey. Below, farther south, in Pembrokeshire, some miles from Tenby, is Manorbier, where the ruins of a thirteenth-century castle overlook the bay.

DUNLUCE CASTLE

Castles in Ireland are numerous and developed on parallel lines to those of England from the twelfth to as late as the seventeenth century. Dunluce Castle in Co. Antrim, Northern Ireland, occupies a romantic position on a rock which is separated from the mainland by a gorge spanned by a bridge. It lies between Bushmills and the seaside resort and port, Portrush, which is also the nearest centre for the Giant's Causeway, that famous series of natural basaltic columns formed out of solidified lava. The rock formation of this coastline has a character of its own and the extensive ruins of Dunluce, with their long and varied line of broken gables, harmonize completely with its somewhat fantastic grandeur. Dunluce was the stronghold of the MacDonnells in the sixteenth century during the reign of Elizabeth. In this turbulent period of Irish history the clans waged war both against each other and against the English government. The Scots-Irish chief, Sorley Boy Mac-Donnell (1505–1590), was active in both respects. However, in 1585 he established himself at Dunluce and in 1586 made submission to Queen Elizabeth's representative and was granted the office of Constable of Dunluce Castle.

ABOVE GLEN BALLYEMON, CO. ANTRIM (right)

The landscape of Ireland is wild and in some districts desolate. Antrim, bounded on the north and east by the narrow seas which separate Ireland from Scotland, has much plateau country sparsely populated, and consisting of heathery moorland and some scattered peat deposits. The plateau of the east slopes gradually down to the valley of the Bann. Some of its characteristics appear in the photograph at right, where white ponies stand on the moors above Glen Ballyemon.

IRISH CABIN, CO. ANTRIM (left)

The stone, white-washed, one-storied cottage is one of the distinctive features of the Irish landscape and its simplicity of form is a sign of the frugal and hard-working life led by the peasants. The interior, however, is often surprisingly spacious, much more so than a glance at the exterior would lead you to suppose. The white walls make a cheerful contrast with the soft and often clouded sky and the mountains which turn deep blue with the distance and atmosphere.

THE VILLAGE SMITHY

Rural Crafts and Occupations

THE British landscape was moulded by men who lived in an agricultural civilization. Britain's greatness was founded not upon industry; not upon coal; but upon the craft of agriculture and in particular upon wool and the sheep that grew that wool. Many of our great country churches were originally wool churches; many of our most beautiful country towns were originally busy market centres. But the craft of agriculture requires tools. It is true to say that the British countryside was moulded by six tools: the axe, the billhook, the chisel, the crook, the plough and the scythe. And these six tools did more than mould the British countryside, they moulded also the British countryman. The men who used those tools took a pride in their work for it was craftsmanship rather than output that was the secret of success. And it was that pride that made Britain beautiful as well as powerful.

Industrialization and particularly mechanization, with its emphasis on mass-production, has made a vast difference in Britain. Industrialization has meant a wholesale migration to the towns. Mechanization (and in some measure, mass-production) has invaded the countryside. The old crafts cannot compete commercially with all this. We do not, nowadays, seem to want things well and beautifully made—made to last; we want them quickly and we want them easily replaced when they wear out. The tempo of modern life is all against craftsmanship. So much so that it is often said that the rural craftsman is dying out.

This is not altogether true. Some of the country trades and crafts of Britain have disappeared within living memory. Others seem doomed to do so. For example, there are, today, few bodgers (or furniture makers) and there are practically no apprentices to this ancient craft. But it is easy to take too gloomy a view. It is true that it is now very difficult to find a good thatcher, very difficult to find a good dry-stone-waller, very difficult to find a man who can make a dew-pond. It is true that the travelling tinker is now a rarity, that basket-makers are not so common as they used to be, that there are fewer blacksmiths since the horse is giving way to the tractor. It is even true that there are fewer full-time professional shepherds — the most skilled of all rural occupations is that of shepherding—than once there were. But then, unfortunately, there are fewer sheep than once there were. All that is true, and it would be easy from a casual survey to draw a very black picture of the future of rural craftsmen. But it is not true that the rural crafts are dying out. The last wood-turner in rural Britain dies, and, behold, there is another in his place! So long as men require houses and ricks to be thatched, there will be men to thatch them, and thatch them as well as did their forefathers. So long as there are horses to be shod, for so long there will be skilled blacksmiths. So long as there are women who wish for hand-woven baskets, for so long will there be men to weave the rushes. So long as there is need for dry-stone walls, men will be found to build them. For so long as British farmers keep sheep, for so long will there be good shepherds. These crafts are part, an essential part, of the life of rural Britain. If they die, rural Britain and the British countryman will die. They will not die, because the British are all countrymen at heart. They are, remember, only a hundred years removed from an agricultural civilization.

All countrymen are not farmers, or farm workers. There are, in the countryside, almost as many trades and occupations as there are in the town. Some, of course, occur in both town and countryside. But the work of the country doctor differs in many respects from that of his urban colleague, and the same is true of the rural veterinary surgeon and the country parson. But there are also many occupations, and skilled occupations at that, that are exclusively rural, and of which much too little is known. Quite apart from those mentioned in the preceding paragraph, there are very considerable numbers engaged in quarrying, in forestry, in brickyards and in fishing. There are a few seasonal occupations which engage the attentions of towns-folk in the fields at the appropriate times. Of these, the best known, but by no means the largest, is hop-picking. Fruit-picking, potato- and sugar-beet-lifting are other examples. Hop-picking, fruit-picking and potato-lifting employ large numbers of women. They cannot, however, be called wholly female occupations. Nor is the traditional dairymaid any longer always female. But weaving, particularly in Cumberland and Northumberland and in Scotland, is truly a countrywoman's work, and happily shows no signs of succumbing to machine competition. Traditional hand-worked lace which used to be done by the women of many villages in the Midlands and the South is now uncommon, though there is yet a fair industry in Buckinghamshire and Nottinghamshire.

Added to these large-scale occupations are many that are scarcely known at all, but which demand great skill on the part of the workers, and which, in return, provide adequate and sometimes generous income. There are, for example, busy ropewalks here and there about the country. There is a considerable net-making industry run on family lines, and so on. And then there is a large number of out-of-the-way occupations and trades. Mole-trapping, coracle-fishing, cockle-gathering, peg-making are examples that come to mind immediately. It needs knowledge to trap moles, skill and courage to manage a coracle; cockle-gathering is not a pursuit for the lazy, and peg-making needs a good eye and firm wrist and considerable powers of concentration. And still up and down the country you will find " mouchers "—men who make a living in a hundred ways, independent men who call no man master, men who are jacks-of-all-trades and masters of most, who will mend a kettle, or trap a mole, or thatch a rick as occasion demands.

But the chief occupation of the countryman today, as in the past, is agriculture. It is too little realized that the farm labourer, often slow of speech and deceptively slow of movement, is a skilled man in a trade that makes great demands on skill and stamina. How many people understand that great skill, infinite patience, and great hardihood are necessary in a good shepherd? A shepherd is much more than a man who watches a flock of sheep. He is at once a good doctor (and he must also have many of the qualities of a good surgeon), a first-class midwife, a skilled weather prophet, a philosopher, a faithful servant, and he must also have the physical strength to spend long hours walking difficult country (should his job be on hilly ground) and the constitution to stand up to long hours in the open in all weathers. A good cowman needs many of the same qualifications. A good ploughman must do more than guide his horses or drive his tractor. The farm labourer, in fact, though he may not always look the part, is a skilled workman in the highest sense of that much abused term.

The British countryman, it is not too much to say, is an experienced, resourceful and ingenious workman, and not infrequently, for tradition dies hard in Britain, he is an excellent craftsman, taking a genuine pride in his work and in his ability to do that work well. But he is rarely assertive, and he is almost always uncommercial.

Experienced, resourceful, and ingenious: exaggerated praise? Not at all; it is no more than the literal truth. Mechanization has invaded the countryside. Tractors displace horses, electricity is used to milk cows and do a hundred-and-one jobs, combine harvesters get bigger and more complicated. The farm labourers who drive the tractors, milk the cows, control the combines, are not mechanics or electricians. They have served no apprenticeship in the workshops. Yet they are excellent mechanics and skilled electricians—self-taught. That is the value of experience and resource. And as to ingenuity, some of the repairs done on tractors that have come to grief miles from farm or village have to be seen to be believed. But they work.

It is easy to become sentimental over the lost glories of the countryside and over the lost status of the country worker and his crafts. Some have died, others have become dimmed. But the life blood of rural Britain flows strongly. The proof of that is to be seen in the adaptability of the countryman. He has shown himself fully equal to dealing with the mechanical devices which have made such changes in agriculture. With all their traditional pride of craft the country folk do not fail to keep abreast of twentieth-century progress.

Tithe Barn. Nothing could better serve as an example of the solid traditional craftsmanship of Britain than the tithe barn with its stone walls and oaken rafters. The magnificent barn shown in the photograph is in Somerset, on a ridge of the Mendips at South Stoke, near Bath.

Britain's Mechanized Agriculture. The twentieth century has witnessed a great revolution in farming methods and by the aid of machinery enormous tracts of land previously lying fallow

or regarded as unsuitable for cultivation have been made to produce bumper harvests. The farm workers have adapted themselves to the four-furrow plough and the combine harvester.

Thrashing (above). The process by which the grain is separated from the husk, once carried out by means of a flail wielded by hand, is now a thoroughly mechanical operation—requiring a number of hands, engine driver, feeder, sack-man and several other men to handle the sheaves, straw, chaff and grain. The straw is restacked on the spot as the work goes on. Thrashing operations are seen in progress on a farm near Bristol in the photograph reproduced above.

Gathering in The Harvest (opposite). Harvest month is the farming festival of the year. The reaper cuts round the ripening wheat, the binder follows and the sheaves are stooked for sun and wind to dry out and bleach both stalk and ear. When sufficiently dried, the sheaves are taken to the thrashing machine. It is an old custom to select a bundle of the best wheat and cheer it.

The Milkmaid. Hand-milking has been largely replaced by mechanical milking devices, but on small farms, the milkmaid on her traditional three-legged stool, is still employed on this work.

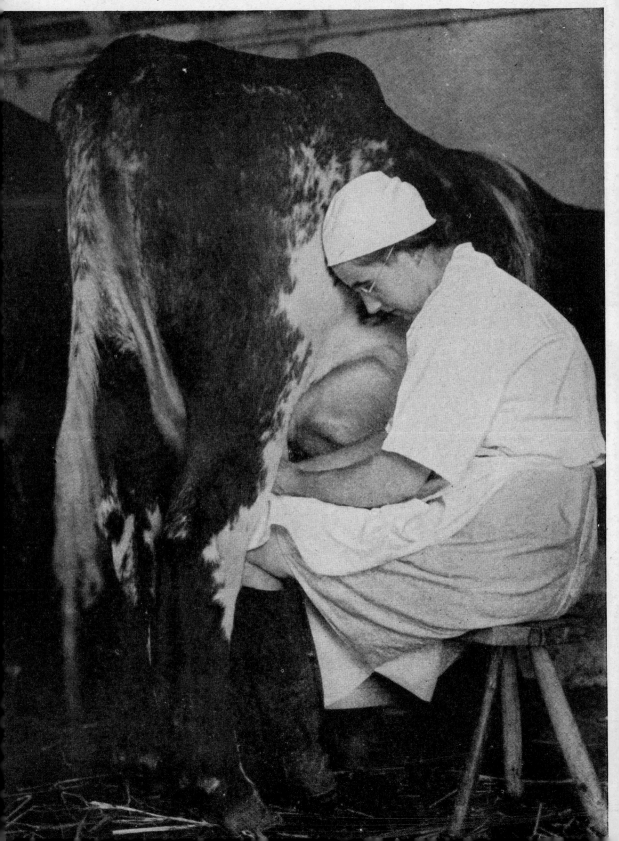

Farm Labourer, Old Style. The sturdy farm labourer shown in the photograph above wears the old-fashioned yoke or wooden collar for carrying his milk pails. Dress and customs change slowly in the British countryside, and this couple at their cottage gate stick to the old ways.

Sheep-shearing. One of the great events of the farming year is sheep-shearing, and the process of hand-clipping is shown above—an operation which requires special skill. The expert leaves

the clipped surface in even ridges, and the evenness and symmetry of these are the sign of his craft. Hand-clipping is widely practised but the use of shearing machines is nowadays widespread.

ANCIENT RURAL INDUSTRIES

At left the wheelwright is seen at work on a job which demands skill and accuracy of a high order. Such industries are often handed down from father to son, and the traditions of the craft are inherited. The blacksmith at right, working in Findon forge, Sussex, comes from a long line of smiths and the forge itself has been in the same family for two hundred years. Below, a horse is shod at the smithy of Crosthwaite, Cumberland.

Stone Quarry (at right). This quarry scene is in the Isle of Portland, on the coast of Dorsetshire. Quarrying is one of the main industries of this island or peninsula (connected with the mainland by Chesil Bank). Portland stone, the oolitic limestone of the region, a rock composed of sea shells consolidated into a mass through the ages, is famous as a building material, many of London's most beautiful buildings owing their surface character to it. Portland cement is so called from its resemblance to Portland stone, but this cement is mainly produced on the Thames and Medway. In our photograph a block of stone is in process of being hauled away from the face of the quarry at Portland.

Building a Stone Wall (below). A Cotswold man places a stone carefully into position in the wall he is building. In this rough form of stonework, irregular pieces of stone are used, usually less than nine inches thick and loosely packed without much regard to courses, the space between large stones being filled in by small ones. This form of walling is much used in stone districts for boundary walls, and the mason works without tools save his hammer and plumb rule to keep his work perpendicular. Rough though the wall is, much skill is required to build durably without using mortar as a binding agent.

Carrying On Tradition. Although the pottery industry of Britain is largely concentrated in Staffordshire, small local potteries still survive. On the left, pots are being placed in the kiln for baking. Below, left, is a stage in cider making. Above is a Welsh countryman, with complete coracle, a boat made of wicker with a leather covering, such as was used by the ancient Britons.

Boatbuilding, Porthleven, Cornwall

The Fraserburgh Herring Fleet. On this and the opposite page are two views of the trawlers of the Fraserburgh herring fleet entering and leaving harbour. Fraserburgh is one of the leading stations of the herring fishery in Scotland and during the herring season which lasts from June to September it has a great influx of population. Its harbour is one of the best on the east coast, covering an area of about thirty acres. Of easy access it affords commodious anchorage for ships.

Trout Nursery (opposite). Fish culture has been highly developed in Britain and here is a scene at a trout nursery in Gloucestershire. The fish are reared in a series of ponds and used for restocking trout streams at regular intervals.

Catch of Northern Waters (below). Scottish girls are busily engaged in dressing and salting herring at Castlebay, the little port of the island of Barra, in the Outer Hebrides, which, remote as it is, trades with the American market.

Repairing a Hedge. One of the most characteristic features of the British countryside is the pattern of hedges which mark the boundaries of its fields, and a great amount of labour goes into their upkeep. When winter comes and other duties are less urgent, the farmer takes the opportunity of putting them to rights. Hedging is in progress here at Lyth, Westmorland.

304

Some Uses of Trees. Above, a couple of country workmen are stripping bark from an oak tree in a Kentish wood, for use in tanyards. Below, picking of withies is in progress in a Somersetshire village. Withies are the supple branches of the variety of willow used in basket-making.

Reed Gathering and Hurdle Making. Above, a load of reeds is being towed home from the Norfolk Broads, and in the picture below, the hurdle maker gives final touches to his work.

Norfolk Thatchers at Work. Thatch has not entirely lost favour as a roofing material although nowadays it is much less common than in the past and thatching is a strictly localized craft. Here, experts from Norfolk are thatching the roof of a modern Kentish inn with reeds from the fens.

Securing the Thatch (opposite). This is the practice of an ancient craft brought up to date, a machine invented and patented nearly half a century ago, contributing to thatch a rick in much less time and at much less cost than by the old hand method. Matting made by this machine can be stored in rolls until harvest time and used promptly when required, cutting out risk of damage by weather. In the photograph mats are being stitched into position.

Basket Making (below). Basketry is extensively practised in Britain, and in addition to articles of furniture, it provides vegetable and fruit baskets, hampers, laundry and linen baskets, etc. It is entirely a handicraft, no machinery at all being used and every stroke has a permanent effect on the structure and symmetry of the finished work. Willow is the material mainly used. The Women's Institutes have adopted the craft and a member is here seen at work.

Two Old Industries. Above is a sailmaker of Rye, Sussex, at work in his loft. The grease horn used for greasing his needle when sewing stiff sail canvas hangs on his belt. He can sew ten yards an hour. Below is a stage in the making of vellum, the calf-skin being scraped and pared.

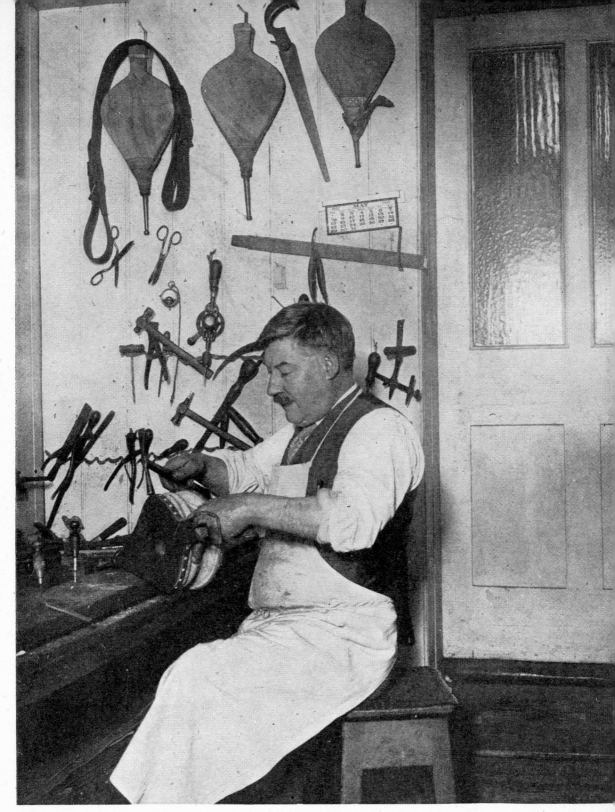

The Bellows Maker. With a goodly array of tools beside and around him, the bellows maker of Crawley, Sussex, is absorbed in his task. He is making secure the leather band which connects the two sides. The leather is kept from collapsing by wire rings which act like the ribs of animals.

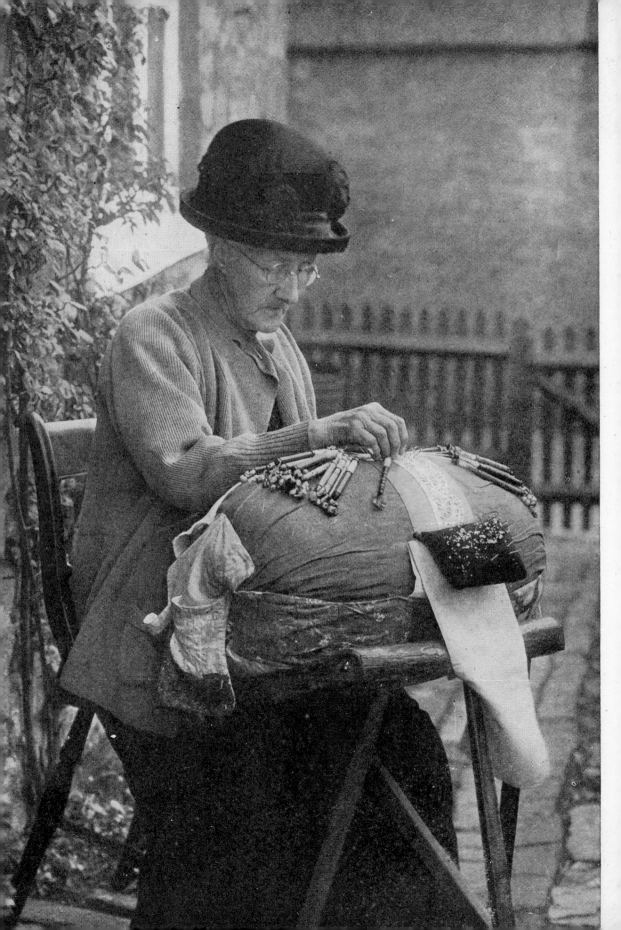

Lace Making (opposite). The lace industry was originally established in Britain by Flemish and Huguenot refugees in the sixteenth century, who settled in the midland counties and in Devon—Honiton lace remaining popular throughout the reign of Queen Victoria; but the rise of the machine and the production of machine-made lace, of course, caused this delicate form of handicraft to dwindle almost to vanishing point. Today it is the fine product of a few devotees of old craftsmanship like this cottage worker at Lavendon, Bucks.

Hebridean Woman at Her Spinning Wheel (below). Spinning, the forming of threads by drawing out and twisting various fibres, was carried out by the most primitive methods until the eighteenth century, when Arkwright, Hargreaves and Crompton invented quicker and mechanical methods. Today, in remote parts of the British Isles, the old hand method, whose results are not surpassed in quality by the machine, is still carried on. Spinning and the succeeding process of hand-weaving constitute a valuable Scottish industry.

Making Besoms. A good, stiff besom still makes an excellent broom and has served that purpose since time immemorial. The word comes from the Old English *besema*, meaning a rod and its most picturesque association is that connected with the witches of the seventeenth century who were supposed to career on their broomsticks about the countryside by night. A Welsh countryman at Pennach in Carnarvonshire, seen in the photograph below, has the bundle of twigs he has collected at his right hand and finished besoms on the left. Concentrated on his task, he is engaged in splitting the hazels which are used for binding firmly round the brooms.

A Chair Bodger at Work. Up to the end of the nineteenth century furniture-making was essentially a craft industry, though little of this still survives. In Buckinghamshire, however, traditionally associated with the making of Windsor chairs (because of the plentiful supply of beech trees in the county) the craft is still carried on apart from machine production. In a primitive-looking hut the quaintly named " bodger " is seen turning the leg of a chair.

315

Tying Strings in the Hopfield. Hop-growing entails setting up a network of string along the forest of poles up which the hops are trained. A farm-worker in one of the many Kentish hopfields is here seen engaged on the task while balancing on the long stilts which are used.

Mending the Nets. A fisherman's net is lightly but strongly made of cotton and care is taken to see that the mesh is sound. At any coastal village one will come across a scene of this kind, where Cornish fishermen are examining and repairing their nets at Sennen Cove near Land's End.

317

Gathering Peat. Plant substances in boggy soil, decomposed and carbonized, when cut and dried, form that useful fuel called peat. It is used mostly in Ireland and Scotland, and these scenes in the Hebrides show, above, stacks of peat; below, an islander of Barra collecting the fuel.

The People of the Shore. Above is a Cornish fisherman with his lobster pots at the village of Penberthy. The pots will be baited with herring and other fish to catch lobsters and crabs. Below, fisherwomen on the Welsh coast are busy gathering cockles in the pools on the sea shore at low tide.

Reaping Scene in Galloway

ACKNOWLEDGMENTS

For permission to use quotations included in this book the Publishers wish to express their thanks to Miss Ruth Pitter, author of Romford Market, and to Messrs. Macmillan for an extract from a poem by T. E. Brown.

S1045 U.   Made and printed by Odhams (Watford) Ltd., Watford